THE COMPLETE MIND MAKEOVER

THE COMPLETE MIND MAKEOVER

TRANSFORM
YOUR LIFE AND
ACHIEVE SUCCESS

ROS TAYLOR

KOGAN PAGE

London and Sterling, VA

Publisher's note

Every possible effort has been made to ensure that the information contained in this book is accurate at the time of going to press, and the publishers and author cannot accept responsibility for any errors or omissions, however caused. No responsibility for loss or damage occasioned to any person acting, or refraining from action, as a result of the material in this publication can be accepted by the editor, the publisher or the author.

Previously published in Great Britain as *Transform Yourself* in 2000 by Kogan Page Limited

First published in Great Britain and the United States as *The Complete Mind Makeover* in 2005 by Kogan Page Limited

120 Pentonville Road
London N1 9JN
United Kingdom
www.kogan-page.co.uk

22883 Quicksilver Drive
Sterling VA 20166-2012
USA

© Ros Taylor, 2005

ISBN 0 7494 4454 1

British Library Cataloguing-in-Publication Data

A CIP record for this book is available from the British Library.

Library of Congress Cataloging-in-Publication Data

Taylor, Ros.
  [Transform yourself!]
  The complete mind makeover : transform your life and achieve success
/ Ros
Taylor.— 1st ed.
    p. cm.
  Originally published: Transform yourself! London : Kogan Page, 2000.
  Includes bibliographical references.
  ISBN 0-7494-4454-1
  1. Self-actualization (Psychology) 2. Success. I. Title.
BF637.S4T396 2005
158—dc22

2005018617

Typeset by Saxon Graphics Ltd, Derby
Printed and bound in Great Britain by Bell & Bain, Glasgow

Contents

About the author

Ros Taylor is a leading UK psychologist, successful business-woman, an accomplished author and a TV and radio presenter. Ros has recently been featured by the *Independent on Sunday* as one of the top 10 coaches in Britain.

Ros travels the world developing the potential of employees through Transform!, a programme she formulated. A creative academic, Ros is a chartered clinical psychologist, coach, trainer and regular speaker on the conference circuit. Newspapers have described her variously as 'the guru of personal development' and 'the best motivational speaker heard this year'.

She has developed a unique style of coaching which achieves major insights and shifts in thinking as well as creating a vision for personal and business success. Ros draws on her background as a psychologist to facilitate creative strategies and move people on to become more than they would ever have believed possible.

Ros broadcasts regularly on radio and has presented a social science research programme *Between Ourselves* for BBC Radio Scotland for two years. She was a presenter for five years on a nightly television news programme. Ros features regularly in the national press and top magazines in her capacity as a psychologist and advisor.

She was one of the three key presenters in *Confidence Lab* for BBC2, a six-part documentary which was broadcast in January 2001. It was her Transform! programme which provided the basis for *Confidence Lab*, and this book outlines its principles. *Fast Track to the Top*, a book about success and how to achieve it, was published by Kogan Page in January 2002.

Ros can be contacted at:

Ros Taylor Ltd
35 St Saviour's Wharf
25 Mill Street
London SE1 2BE
Tel: 020 7231 3659
e-mail: ros@rostaylor.com
www.rostaylor.com

Introduction and overview of the book

Max Bryce was a self-made man. He delighted in saying that no one had ever helped him on his way to the top. As head of his IT firm he travelled the world attending sales conferences. He could have sent his sales team but he didn't believe they could handle the big contracts. He was equally critical of his wife and family and would fly into rages if there was even the slightest mark on the kitchen floor from dogs or children. He was a perfectionist and proud of it.

On one of his international trips he contracted a virus and as he was rushed home to receive specialist care, he gradually became blind. Suddenly he had to depend on his family for his every need and his employees to continue the business he had started.

He changed. He had to slow down, trust others to help him, listen and become more sensitive to his family. His eyesight returned but the experience never left him. Relationships with those around him became as important as the success of the company – and the surprising thing was that the balance sheet never looked better.

People transformed from bad to good are the stuff of life, celebrated in newspaper articles, novels and films. But does that metamorphosis have to take place so traumatically?

Charles Handy, the business guru, writes that sometimes the trauma shocks us out of our routine existence and when we are uncomfortable then change can take place. He tells a story about frogs. You have probably heard it. If you put a frog in water and bring it very gradually to the boil – although I can't imagine why you would ever want to do that – the frog won't jump out and save itself. Presumably, a quick burst of heat would have the frog leaping to freedom.

There are, of course, other ways to change apart from the threat of being boiled alive. Luckily books help us to reappraise ourselves or at least think differently. It helps that a major drive for human beings is to aspire to perfection. However, this is countered by an equally powerful desire to do nothing about it. Tapping into this drive, 'how to' books are published in their millions. Some are read, digested and acted upon; others languish unopened on bookshelves, as if buying them were sufficient.

It's really not that easy to change. Many otherwise intelligent people firmly believe you can't. This view is often held by those who are keen to remain the same – the same lovable swine they have always been. Reflecting on how they might have changed over the years can reveal a gradual degeneration into swinehood rather than having swinehood genetically thrust upon them. So they do change – just not in the right direction.

It helps of course if you can invest some time and effort in doing things differently. Buying the book in itself is not enough. Even reading it will not suffice. You will need to become experimental, trying some of the suggestions to see if they work for you. Then try some more. In the film 'Groundhog Day', the hero had the unusual luxury of re-running the same scene again and again until he got it right; he became emotionally competent and got the girl. So, in the acquisition of new skills, repetition is key. It takes three weeks to replace an old habit with a new skill and at least another nine weeks to turn that new skill into a new habit – not that long really, if you've had the bad habit for 20 years.

Many participants on courses and one-to-one coaching sessions have complained that they feel uncomfortable with the new skills of, for example, selling themselves at interview or using compliments more freely. They know they ought to do these things, but they don't come naturally. The process of acquiring the skills contained in this book is just the same as learning to drive, play golf or speak French fluently. Don't tell me you were instantly successful or comfortable with these. I bet it took time, occasional successes, more frequent failures and gradual improvements to progress.

This book is for anyone seeking self-development and for those at work who desire promotion or, if professionally or technically qualified, would like more proficient people skills. There is so much competition for each job now that technical qualifications to a high standard are taken for granted. So an employer cannot fail to be impressed by candidates who can prove, for example, that they can think creatively, have captivating interpersonal skills and can handle conflict elegantly.

Organizations and change

You don't need me to tell you how organizations have changed. You are working or have worked in them. They are less secure places than they used to be, with less staff, more targets, more competition, more stress.

Downsizing and restructuring have left organizations with fewer levels of authority and no traditional chain of command. All of this could be hugely exciting, permitting younger members of staff to become more influential in terms of ideas, product development and customer contact. People on the shop floor could run manufacturing lines themselves, increasing their stimulation and leaving managers with more thinking and planning time. Sadly for many (dare I say most) organizations this freeing from the shackles of an authoritarian structure has been a mixed blessing or not a blessing at all.

Companies in pursuit of maximum profit and minimum overheads change systems, technology, structure and manpower almost constantly. And the rallying cry is 'learn to love change or die'.

Consultant colleagues may have made fortunes with total quality management, business process re-engineering, and management 'fads', but a review from a student at the London

School of Economics reports that all these measures have failed to change organizations in any lasting or profound way. Employees are not fools. They know that CEOs are brought in for a couple of years to effect change and then leave. So they learn the jargon, keep their heads down and do as little as possible. They will still be there long after the current boss has gone and a new management fad has materialized.

Consultants are brought in to handle a specific project, such as the introduction of a new manufacturing system. From this involvement they may then extrapolate their ideas for organizational change and if the company is lucky and the consultants are earning their money the implications for team functioning may be considered.

What all of these projects fail to do is give individual employees the skills to deal with the changes of a flat-structured, downsized company. Abandoning levels of management means you can't tell people what to do, as the chances are they are on the same level as you. A whole new set of techniques is necessary. Never before have the skills of motivating and influencing been so important. *The Complete Mind Makeover* can supply you with these skills, help you to recapture personal motivation, learn the secret of motivating others, handle difficult people elegantly and solve problems creatively.

About the book

There are loads of other self-help books on the market, many of which I wish I had written myself. The majority focus on one or perhaps two aspects of the personal change process, which for some people is enough leverage to change. A favourite of mine is *Being Happy* by Andrew Matthews. The following quote had quite a profound emotional effect on me and helped me focus on life's priorities at a time when I needed that reminder. I just have to show you what I mean. The piece was written by an 85-year-old man who learnt that he was dying. It is particularly relevant.

> If I had my life to live over again, I'd try to make more mistakes next time. I wouldn't be so perfect. I would relax more. I'd

limber up. I'd be sillier than I've been on this trip. In fact, I know very few things that I would take so seriously. I'd be crazier. I'd be less hygienic.

I'd take more chances, I'd take more trips, I'd climb more mountains, I'd swim more rivers, I'd go places I've never been to. I'd eat more ice cream and fewer beans.

I'd have more actual troubles and fewer imaginary ones!

You see, I was one of those people who live prophylactically and sensibly and sanely hour after hour and day after day. Oh, I've had my moments, and if I had it to do over again, I'd have more of those moments – moment by moment by moment.

I've been one of those people who never went anywhere without a thermometer, a hot water bottle, a gargle, a raincoat and a parachute. If I had it to do all over again, I'd travel lighter next time.

If I had it to do all over again, I'd start barefoot earlier in the spring and stay way later in the fall. I'd ride more merry-go-rounds, I'd watch more sunrises, and I'd play with more children, if I had my life to live over again.

But you see I don't.

I remember reading – it was in the *Evening Standard* I think – that the golfer Nick Faldo had been given a copy of *Being Happy* by his coach and it completely changed his life. Those who follow golf will know he had been an unapproachable person, often refusing to sign autographs for fans and being pretty churlish generally. The photograph in that paper had captured him smiling exuberantly on the catwalk of a charity fashion show. A changed man indeed.

A more behaviourally targeted book is *How to Win Friends and Influence People*, by Dale Carnegie. Written in 1938 it is still the best book on the market about interpersonal skills. The concept of making other people feel important if you want to influence them is so powerful it led me to rethink the whole philosophy of assertiveness and the way I interacted with people at work and at home.

What I have set out to do in this book is to explore the latest experience in personal change so that all angles are covered, not just emotion or action but also how we impact on people and our thought processes. Any one of these can effect change, but if you can follow the process of all four elements, the odds of changing are increased immeasurably. The chapters of the book follow the makeover model shown in Figure I.1. I will outline the steps so that you get a feel for the book's intentions.

Step 1
Impact
How to create a good first impression

Before a single word is uttered, we are aware of the impact others have on us. Human beings can construct quite sophisticated judgements about people they may only have seen at a distance, or have not even met. By the same token we have that effect on others. The first chapter concentrates on the impact of first impressions, the trust (or lack of it) we feel for some people, and the body language signals we pick up and emit. Apparently this gut level, emotional reaction precedes any thought process; the 'there's just something about them' that repels or attracts.

An example of someone who markedly changed the first impressions he made on others was a client called Jack. When he arrived at our offices he made no greeting to any of us, simply announced he had an important call to make and

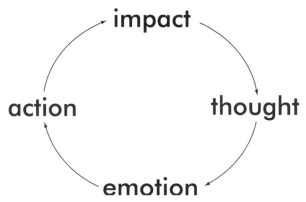

Figure I.1

barged his way to the nearest telephone. I know from talking to him afterwards that he had no idea how we felt about him and his arrival. ('Arrogant, egotistical swine' were some of the more printable epithets from our administrator.) Of course he went through his training and thankfully changed but you can imagine the needless hostility he must have encountered in the past when visiting colleagues and clients.

How we come across initially to others is due in no small part to *body language*. The nature of captivating non-verbal skills will be discussed to help you get that job promotion or, equally if not more important, that partner for life. Of course the excitement of studying body language is not just the analysis of someone else's actions but also of your own in response – endlessly diverting when you're waiting in stations and airport terminals.

Motivation underpins everything. Without it we are as dull as dishwater. So this chapter will also look at what motivates you, allowing you to assess what drives you using the 'career drivers' survey. It is so important to know what rewards us, as when we move jobs or go for promotion we have to make sure the new post has all the motivators to keep us enthusiastic. Promotion is not enough.

Also key is understanding how we can motivate or demotivate others. Generally we think that everyone is the same as us and judge him or her accordingly. Excitingly this is not true. For instance, you may suggest inviting a visiting expert from America to take a look at the department and perhaps run it for a while. Late in the day you realize that a colleague is driven by power and expertise, and you will need to think of a clever way of selling this idea as you now have one demotivated member of staff who thought he or she was running the show as the resident expert.

The other element in this section is about having fun and loving what you do, enjoying the process, not just the status or money at the end of it. Millionaires are always looking for glitches in systems, new deals, new horizons. They like the stimulation of it all. What stimulates and excites you? This chapter will help you with that discovery.

Step 2
Thought
How to develop a variety of thinking styles

Much has been written about thought, mental attitude, belief – call it what you will. And most of what we hear sounds suspiciously over the top with admonitions to think positively no matter what the circumstances might be. Personally, I rather like to be reminded to have a nice day just in case I might forget that one was on offer. And it beats hands down the grunt and glare treatment from a few still untrained shop assistants.

But the whole positive thinking, mental attitude lobby has always seemed simplistic to me. As a psychologist, I understand the importance of cognitions in shaping our lives, but the idea that we should feel positive *all* the time, even in a crisis, has always seemed laughable. There needs to be a choice of thinking styles to suit the occasion. The interviewees in a pilot group for another book I co-authored, *Fast Track to the Top*, have mentioned problem-solving abilities as one of the major talents they admired in their role models. Analysis of what problem solvers do is encapsulated in *outcome thinking*. This chapter will examine such thinking as a skill that can be acquired, with lots of examples of people who utilized outcome thinking in a crisis.

I will examine, with case studies, how the way we think can hold us back and put a ceiling on our aspirations. Changing, of course, is not easy. We must catch ourselves using negative language about work, colleagues and organizations and ask ourselves how useful this thinking is in reaching our goals.

Reality thinking is a way to test the veracity of our thinking. It is about examining the evidence for beliefs and challenging automatic thoughts from the past. These thoughts may have sprung up from childhood and may be long past their sell-by date. If you can identify some of these in yourself, you can ditch them and move on.

Of course there is a time for *positive thinking*. When we are looking towards future goals or visualizing success, then thinking positively can work splendidly. There will be an opportunity in this chapter for you to experience a more positive thinking style and goal planning.

A large piece of long-term research into thinking styles was carried out by Seligman, a US psychologist. He tapped phones, gathered letters and memos and had researchers listen in to coffee-time chat. He then analysed the results in terms of positive and negative language and extrapolated that to thinking style. Following up his subjects over 25 years (at least it was 25 when I heard him speak) he discovered that more positive thinkers lived longer, had fewer nasty life events happen to them, were more successful and were less likely to become depressed. That evidence worked for me. I have worked at thinking more positively ever since.

Step 3
Emotion
How to develop your emotional intelligence

Sir John Harvey-Jones once commented at an Institute of Directors conference that Tina Knight of Nighthawk Communications had 'passion'. What he meant was that she was emotional about her business and vociferous in her love of entrepreneurship.

Success cannot be acquired by technical skills alone. You have to inspire, communicate and wow people internal and external to the organization. This ability is called *emotional intelligence* (EQ). This chapter explores the five domains of EQ and talks about how to become emotionally intelligent.

When I was training, psychologists were beavering away to find a link between IQ and later success in life and were being confounded. Now the concept of EQ is achieving significant results, correlating highly with the ability to succeed. I think we always knew that it's not what you have but what you do with it that counts. Proving it was just a little more difficult.

There are huge differences between men and women in handling emotion. Men want to resolve upsets and issues by themselves, emerging triumphant from a whole lot of cogitation. Women talk, and as they talk, reach conclusions and solutions. Understanding these differences will become increasingly important as more women reach senior levels in organizations.

Eric Berne's concept of *stroking* will be discussed with some reflection on your life and who you choose and don't choose to reward and compliment. The impact of recognition of any sort is so great that staff become slaves to managers and leaders who stroke genuinely. You too can engender this loyalty if you follow the guidelines offered.

I remember a friend of mine, a prominent Scottish businesswoman, telling me that there was no room for emotion in business. That may have been wishful thinking because, in my experience, work is a teeming hotbed of often unexpressed emotion. How elegantly we handle that emotion will determine the nature of our relationships. An 'emotional coaching' questionnaire will assess your ability to handle a variety of emotions in others.

Step 4
Action
How to change your behaviour and improve your people skills

Self-awareness, motivation, positive thinking, emotional intelligence, all come to naught unless we can act differently. The old adage about actions speaking louder than words is true.

I remember a company where I worked as a consultant, deciding to embark on a total quality management programme. They had spent an enormous amount of money on set-up costs and a launch to which all employees were invited. The managing director stood on a platform and announced that total quality was the concern of every individual and the management of this organization would be walking about. 'Believe me,' he cried, 'this will not be the last time you see me.' But it was. The staff had never met him before and so had not missed him. Now they knew who he was and were all too aware of his absence from their lives. His 'all talk and no action' philosophy sadly made employees cynical about the whole programme. A little tangential aside – the leaflets they had printed for the launch were entitled 'Total *Quailty* Management'. A bad start from which the project never recovered.

So this chapter will be about doing things or behaving differently. For example, *handling difficult* people in an organization is a core skill, because 'difficult' people are often the most motivated employees. All that energy put into disagreeing could, with a bit of planning, be put to positive use. So we will indulge in a bit of behavioural analysis of your pet difficult person, adding a dash of personal perception and proceeding with a glorious philosophical overview that will revolutionize your interpersonal skills. Then the challenge – you must put these new skills into practice or you will not be made over.

If difficult people have been that way for quite some time and you have tried every trick in the book to change them, then you need the DESC script – describe, emotion, solutions, consequences. Wonderful for last ditch attempts when all else has failed. Of course there are no guarantees of success but these skills definitely increase the odds in your favour.

In general, what we are looking at here is a planned and graduated response to people issues and challenges rather than just shooting from the hip or avoiding difficult people, hoping they will disappear. In companies much midnight oil is burnt in financial planning and projecting, reviewing the latest information technology or reorganizing the management structure. But when it comes to motivating staff or dealing with conflict, the response is usually knee-jerk, with little planning and forethought.

Marion Bell, a lawyer with whom I run courses for Industrial Relations Services, often remarks that if more managers, team leaders and supervisors were more skilled in how they deal with the difficult, upset or stressed employee, then litigation would be minimized.

So now that you know where you are going, fasten your seat belt – you are about to embark on a complete mind makeover.

Step 1

Impact

How to create a good first impression

First impressions

First impressions can profoundly affect potential relationships, either encouraging them or putting us off for life.

So how do you come across to others when you first meet? This self-awareness is difficult to achieve since you can hardly ask that new friend, colleague or client 'How did I come across to you just now when we were introduced?' Well, you could, but not without being labelled slightly strange and neurotic.

Can we remember dynamic or captivating first impressions? I was musing on some for the purpose of this book, when I recalled meeting Aaron Beck, the father of cognitive psychology. Before his arrival on the academic scene, psychologists were focused on studying only behaviour that could be seen or measured; 'thinking' did not count. He changed all that at a stroke, by declaring that in fact thoughts were behaviours worthy of study and measurement. And he revealed in the 1970s how depression and anxiety could be improved by the careful examination and changing of the thought patterns he called 'automatic thoughts'. I mention all this to give credibility to his guru-like status among psychologists. I suppose I expected someone arrogant and opinionated, but this man was charming and interested in others. He asked about the private practice I had at the time, sharing anecdotes of difficult cases. He must have been over 70, fit and lively, but of even more importance, intellectually sharp. New ideas still enthralled him. All this was impactful enough, but when I met him again a few years later in another city he recalled our first meeting in Glasgow. Heady stuff from a famous man.

Quite the reverse was true of an encounter with Martin Amis in a television studio where I worked as a presenter. I had just finished reading his latest novel and wanted to check that the main protagonists were in fact dead from the beginning. He fixed me a look of such disdain a worm would have fared better, saying 'Of course they were dead'. I wanted to say in my defence that it really was quite unusual to have dead people doing lively and non-ghostly things throughout a book and that at least I had read it, which was more than could be said for the guy who interviewed him. But I remained mute and more than slightly humiliated.

Two encounters: one enhancing, the other detracting.

If I produced a rating scale with 'enhancing' at one end with 10 points, and 'detracting' at the other with 0, where would you come on that scale right now? And where would you like to be? If you are a Martin Amis who works alone as a writer, then you can perhaps afford a 0 rating, though I'm sure it must damage the relationships he does have. For the rest of us who collaborate with or manage others we have to aspire to a rating of 10.

Daniel Goleman, in his book *Emotional Intelligence*, firmly places this gut reaction, these trust/non-trust feelings we experience, at the core, the very genesis of interpersonal communication. A bump in the night can have us shooting out of bed before we realize what caused it – cat or cat burglar? But at the same time this gut reaction can make us wary of dangerous or boring people, or drawn to those with whom we feel comfortable or stimulated.

Discover the impact you make by constructing a 30-second commercial about you. In the space below write a brief advert describing what talents and skills you bring to your organization, department or life in general. Take no more than five minutes to prepare it and then take exactly 30 seconds to read it through.

Your 30-second commercial

Now ask yourself the following questions:

1. When talking through your commercial was the language you used positive, talking about strengths, or did some weaknesses sneak in?
2. Did you use qualifying words like 'fairly' good at…, 'quite' organized…, or I 'think' people would say I was…?
3. Thirty seconds is not a long time, but did you utilize it well? Or had you just started when the thirty seconds were up?
4. Did you use buzzwords when you were making notes, or long sentences that took up too much time?

This exercise is not something you would choose to do in real life. Boasting about your strengths is seen as, well, boasting! However, if someone asks you at a party what you do, what is your reply? Do you sell yourself? Is your answer crisp, pithy and to the point, or do you ramble on in a slightly apologetic fashion?

Just declaring what you are good at does not have to be over the top. You are not saying you are the world's best or the greatest thing since sliced bread. Just good. Two major points to remember:

■ It takes 30 seconds or less to make a good first impression and about 5 to make a bad one.
■ The lion's share of promotions are achieved through doing a job well, and also through being seen to do a job well.

Find a positive way to sell what you do in short, crisp sentences. Practise it at every opportunity when you meet a new person.

Body language

Of course how you look when you talk is of primary importance. Despite knowing how crucial *body language* is in terms of impact (if not look at Mehrabian's chart in Figure 1.1), we still focus on content too much of the time – what we say, not how we say it. I think Mehrabian's estimate of 55 per cent is

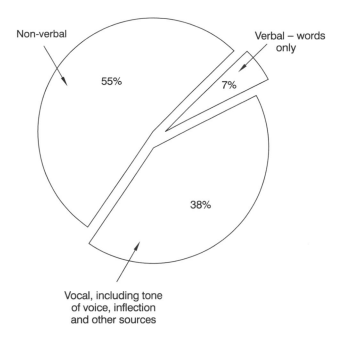

Figure 1.1

conservative as other researchers suggest the impact of body language is nearer 80 per cent of communication. Suffice it to say it's important!

I was looking through Allan Pease's book *Body Language* for inspiration before being interviewed on television about Monica Lewinsky's body language with President Clinton. In the first chapter I was reminded how profoundly visual we are, which is why body language is so crucial. Pease cites Professor Birtwhistell's estimate of 10 to 11 minutes of conversation for the average person per day, with sentences lasting on average a mere 2.5 seconds. The rest is non-verbal. Certainly Monica was communicating pretty powerfully without words to Bill in the clip I had to analyse. Lots of intimate direct gaze followed by hooded eyes scanning his body.

There is a view that body language reveals the hidden person, the unconscious impulse, mainly because we can 'choose our words carefully' but tend not to think of controlling

INSIGHT

At an opera competition a number of years ago there was a constellation of talent promised. The programme commenced with a more than competent tenor who chose the famous aria from 'Don Giovanni'. This was followed by a rather luscious coloratura soprano. How could anyone choose between them? The judges were pitied. There then appeared another tenor who came to the front of the stage and enacted for the audience an aria by Mozart, which seemed somehow familiar. He was superb: passionate, amusing, teasing, flirtatious by turns. He moved around the stage, his gestures all-encompassing, his facial expressions captivating. He stole the show and finished to a standing ovation. On the way home I looked at the programme to see what he had been singing. No wonder it had been familiar – it was exactly the same aria the first tenor sang. Ridiculous not to have realized it but in his hands it had become a different song, a different communication. Objectively, the first guy probably had a better voice but his body language had been minimal with no expression and therefore no oomph. No oomph, no success.

our body language. This was revealed to me anew when I took part in yet another television programme, 'The Unconscious Mind'. The producer decided he wanted to monitor people in party mode to see if a team of observers (some colleagues and myself) could deduce what their interactions were all about, without verbal input.

The BBC pushed the boat out with alcoholic beverages and things on sticks. Our participative audience knew that the programme was about non-verbal communication but they were told they had to converse for five minutes with at least four new people and remember what they discovered. This instruction seemed sufficient to divert attention from their actions, and five cameras picked up nuances in their behaviour. We had a cross-section of employees of varying ages from microelectronics, manufacturing and service industries, as well as a number of unemployed people.

In general I was struck by the qualities which had dynamic impact on television. The most beautiful were not necessarily the most outstanding in terms of visual appeal. Energy, facial mobility and expressiveness were infinitely more captivating. At the opposite end of the spectrum was a young guy who constantly touched his face – a pull at his ear lobe then a rub of the eye, an index finger under the nose. This was accompanied by poor eye contact and a lot of looking at the floor.

During the feedback session at the end of the programme I mentioned this habit of his and his surprise was complete. Poor soul, while he was denying ever possessing these traits he was touching his nose and tugging at his ear. When the audience shouted out 'You're doing it now', he looked at his hand as if it were attached to someone else. I asked if he had always been as shy and socially embarrassed. He then confided that he had been unemployed for about two years and had no money to socialize, so this gathering had been very daunting for him. As observers, this had been so obvious to us and since we were all psychologists we quite inappropriately wanted to take him home and mother him.

Another programme participant needing absolutely no mothering was Peter. I had noticed he only chose women to talk to and had quite compelling body language. When the audience were asked who they enjoyed talking to most, his name was mentioned regularly. Reviewing the programme tapes, time and again we were drawn to him. He smiled a lot, his eye contact was direct and entirely focused on the person he was conversing with. This was in no way ingratiating. He simply looked as if he loved talking to people, especially female people. Despite being quite short in stature he was confident, moving back and forth on the balls of his feet on some occasions. A listener more than a talker, he got close to his partners, almost touching but not quite. The women he chose responded to his attention like flowers to sunlight, becoming sparkling and animated with increased smiling and gesturing. I could hear through my earpiece the producer and colleagues jealously asking who this creep was and how did he get so many women to look so adoring. A glance round the studio would have told them he was different. Other men were talking and not listening, their eye contact ranging around the room to other people and beyond. Women were listening to conversations that had, one could only surmise, very little relevance to them as their feet tapped, hair was touched and nails appraised or eyes scanned the horizon for more interesting contacts.

When feeding back to the audience at the end of the programme, I complimented Peter on his interpersonal skills, especially with women. For the first time he looked uncomfortable, shifting around in his seat as I mentioned this to him. Then he revealed that he was getting married in two weeks' time and his fiancée was in the audience. The entire group sympathized with her. 'I'd watch that one', 'He'll be a handful', etc were uttered while the guys in the gallery took notes on his strategies – strategies so simple that I wonder why we don't carry them out more regularly when meeting people, especially for the first time.

Peter's strategies

1. Smile.
2. Eye contact riveted when someone is talking.
3. Nodding approval.
4. Lots of listening.
5. Smile again.

What stops us carrying out such seemingly simple strategies when we know they work so powerfully? Is it life, stress, absorption with our own agendas, or just not caring? If you are going to embark on a mind makeover, you must care about the people around you – not just your intimate circle of friends and relations – but everyone: colleagues, acquaintances, people you have just met.

When I was at university (a good few years ago now, it must be said), the two principals in the Department of Philosophy wrote a book called *Respect for Persons*. I had not wanted to take the subject (apparently I needed it to complete my degree) but ended up loving it. For a year we discussed heatedly, in and out of tutorials, things like the nature of humanity, what is honesty and why we should have respect for people. The arguments are lost in the mists of time and alcohol but the principles linger on. What I remember most was that people are 'ends' in themselves not 'means to ends'. People should be cherished and helped to flourish.

In all our dealings with others in our families, social life, at work, on street corners, on buses, we have to regard the supreme worth of the individual person. The full implication of this philosophy hit me one day travelling on a commuter train from Waterloo to Guildford. The ticket inspector asked politely for my ticket and I handed it over without even looking at him. I just kept on reading. Of course what that signalled to him was that *me* and my book were more important than he was. And this from me who believes in the worth of everyone. My body language belied my beliefs.

This happens so much in companies where ascendancy seems directly correlated with increased pontificating, less eye contact, more telling than asking. The effect on staff is incalculable and thoroughly demeaning.

Let me give you an example of when I visited a chief medical officer of a large pharmaceutical company – at his request, I may say. He welcomed me to his office and talked to me about the organization, especially his role in it. It was all a tad arrogant, but there was nothing too unusual about that. However, when I was telling him the background of my company and the services we provide he ceased to look at me. At first I thought he was writing notes, which might have excused him somewhat, but he was in fact doodling. The effect it had was to shut me up. I slowed down and gradually lost enthusiasm. Then I went to the other extreme and started saying quite outrageous things just to get him to look up. He never did, and surprise, surprise, we never worked together. What he did was discount me, made me feel unimportant by not engaging and involving me. God help the staff who worked for him. He is probably complaining even as I write that you can't get good, motivated staff nowadays.

It all seems so obvious that you just cannot imagine people not knowing how they come across to others, but they really have no idea. And the more senior they are in a company, the less anyone provides feedback.

As organizations de-layer and downsize the outcome is less authority, less formality. People used to hiding behind status and roles can feel confused as to how they should act.

I was coaching a manager of a microelectronics company in Scotland recently to improve her presentation skills. She gave a good workmanlike performance but was very stiff and formal. When we looked at the video she confided that she had developed this image to gain respect, but was in fact more than a little 'wild' at home. Wild to me implies energy, creativity, fun, none of which she felt able to show at work, and work was the loser. We decided she could relax her body language when she stood to speak by leaning on the edge of a table or chair, using larger gestures, smiling more. The effect was to enliven her and permit her to become herself.

I know that many of you are brought up with the concept of being 'professional'. To many accountants, lawyers, engineers and doctors, this seems to be an excuse not just to be serious but to be stiff and boring. Becoming that way takes a lot of practice and what a waste of time! Hands behind the back, eyes to the ceiling, read from the text and your audience is either wondering what to have for lunch or is already dozing off. Whoever told us that when faced with a large audience or at least one of more than ten people we should change from being a normal chatty person to a rigid cardboard cutout? And it is not just nerves. This formality has been elevated to a philosophy of professional behaviour that pervades entire organizations, so most meetings, presentations and conferences have to be endured rather than enjoyed.

There is a wonderfully simple rule about all of this. When you are 'yourself' your body language is congruent with your message, which means that what you say and how you look are fused into one powerful communication with no distractions. You also come across as genuine and honest, something we would all wish to achieve.

Just as important as an awareness of our own body language is our ability to perceive and react to other people's. It is particularly useful to know if a client, customer, or boss is interested in what we are saying or if they have switched off. Take a look at Figure 1.2 and try to imagine he is at a presentation you are making.

■ How is he receiving your ideas?
■ What in the body language lets you know?
■ What would you do about it?

Figure 1.2

- This body language is known as 'The common critical evaluation cluster'.
- Arms and legs are tightly crossed, a frown is on his face with a hand over his mouth as if he can't quite trust himself to speak because if he did, he would be damning.
- His body is also positioned side-on to you, revealing scepticism and a desire to opt out.

If, when you are speaking, you are confronted with someone looking like this, you ignore the signs at your peril. You must intervene with some questions, not with the purpose of punishment as in 'Stop your horrible body language', but to discover why they are in disagreement with you. If you don't they will probably be thinking about some statistic in your first slide and will not have heard a word you have said since.

Here are some possible interventions you might want to try. Note that they are non-confrontational and focus on you the communicator being at fault for not being clear, not the listener. When you do intervene, what is truly amazing is that the body language of your listener changes immediately, even before they reply.

Possible questions

- Is everything all right?
- You seem a little unsure of what I've said.
- What can I clarify for you?
- You look distracted. What's wrong?
- I'm not sure I've made myself clear. What can I do to help?

Another way of changing someone's body language to a more agreeable position is suggested by neuro-linguistic programming (NLP). Proponents suggest that when we copy or mirror another's body language we reveal to them without words that we understand them. I'll give you an example to help explain.

I was working for a plastics company near Manchester, carrying out a training needs analysis for their senior managers. The Finance Director was first on my list for interviewing. As soon as I entered the room he challenged me with 'I hope you are not going to take long as I can only spare you 10 minutes.' Big desk, plant, black leather executive chair – the whole authoritarian works. Behind his desk he was leaning forward, hands clasped tightly so I leant forward too. Gradually during the interview I moved back in my seat, slowed down my speech, used open gestures, smiled more and magically so did he. The outcome – I was there for two hours and we parted the best of friends. What I did was this:

- *Mirrored* – I copied his body language roughly (not slavishly), leaning forward, hands clasped.
- *Changed pace* – I slowed down my pace in order to relax him. He probably felt threatened that a training needs analysis would show that he required training, which of course it did. But by this time he minded less as his comfort had increased.
- *Led* – I moved into my increasingly more relaxed position very slowly to allow him to follow my lead.

In a business context it is important to understand what some particular non-verbal cues mean so that you can take appropriate action. A warning though: you must look for body language clusters, not isolated bits of behaviour. If you look back to the critical evaluation cluster (page 23) for example, you will notice that a variety of signals comprise this behaviour. So perceive carefully and remember you can always check it out because it is, after all, only 50 to 80 per cent of communication. Other information is important too. The list overleaf will help you make a start on becoming *a body language sleuth.*

Motivators

Still linked to impact is *motivation.* If someone is motivated, they are lively, energetic, enthusiastic and in turn motivational. It is

Body language sleuthing

NON-VERBAL CUES	POSSIBLE PROCESSES
Furrowed forehead, knitted brows	Thinking, perhaps not positively
Tapping foot and/or drumming fingers	Impatience, irritation, anger, agitation
Avoiding eye contact	Anger, concern, sexual attraction
Rapid, light breathing	Anxiety, fear, distress
Irregular breathing	Approaching important issues, controlling feelings
Deep, slow breathing	Suppressing strong feelings
Controlled, low, quiet voice	Suppressing energy/interest, excitement
Fast, high voice	Excitement, tension, fear
Tightness/rigidity in jaw, neck, shoulder	Holding back anger or upset
Clenching fists, tightness in arm	Holding back anger or upset
Body leaning forward, legs tightly crossed	Defending, uninvolved, unconcerned
Arms tightly folded, legs tightly crossed	Defending, putting up barriers, resistance
Lounging extravagantly in chair	Detachment, cynicism, discounting
Hand covering mouth	Hiding, playing games, uncertain
Finger jabbing	Critical, putting down, fencing with

Positive body language

Smiling	Happy, confident, at ease
Direct gaze	Nothing to hide, confident in relationships
Head erect, good posture	High self-esteem
Open gestures	Open, honest person
Head to one side	Listening positively
Leaning forward	Interested in what is being said
Nodding	Approval of another person's point of view

one of life's certainties that you cannot inspire if you are not yourself inspired.

I was sitting last week in one of those glass offices of a Scottish microelectronics company when the European director arrived. Their year-end figures, predicted to be excellent, turned out to be less startling. This guy flung himself through the door in a mixture of anger, irritation and depression.

I could hear nothing through the glass but the finger pointing and the resultant dispirited body language in the assembled staff spelt blame and upset where there had been energy before. Did he really think he was motivating them? He was pissed off so he pissed them off. Before noon, morale in the whole plant was at an all-time low just when they should have been energetically problem solving. 'I kicked ass' he will proudly state to his US masters, having demotivated the entire workforce. If only this kind of punishment worked, we could hold flagellation classes – individual and group. But of course it doesn't.

Let's reflect on motivators and demotivators in our own lives. Try answering the questions below, describing not only the people and circumstances but specifically what they did or what happened. Try reflecting initially on your early years. Did your parents motivate you? What about an elder brother or sister, relative or friend? Then think about school, sport, hobbies, college or university, your first job. Who or what at that time motivated or demotivated you?

My way exercise

- Who or what has motivated you?
- Who or what has demotivated you?
- Whom have you motivated?
- Whom have you demotivated?

This exercise helps to focus on what has happened to us and should generate a 'do as you would be done by' philosophy.

And it should be clear that people even more than circumstances provide motivation and direction in our lives.

But it has also been my experience that we are much more aware of who has motivated us and demotivated us than whom we have motivated and demotivated. We keenly feel the put-downs and exult in the praise but when it comes to others, well, it's a bit of a memory lapse. Let's start with you personally, then later in the chapter we will discuss what we do to others and why we can get it so wrong.

When I embarked on this chapter, I foolishly thought that few people had motivated me during my life and any success I had achieved had been as a result of my own endeavours. But as I contemplated upbringing, sport, hobbies, work and even this book, I realized how ridiculous was my notion of myself as a 'self-made woman'. The people who have motivated me are:

NAME	HOW THEY MOTIVATED ME
Winifred Busfield – singing teacher	Infinite praise, constructive criticism, support at even minor concerts, and glorious wackiness.
Mr Lemon – swimming teacher	Caring, patient. First man I fancied.
Philip Gardner – psychology lecturer	Made learning psychology fun.
Iain Kennedy – MD, Solectron	Keen interest in training and coaching I do for his staff. Phones to thank me every time.
John Dent – personal trainer	Praise for even the slightest improvements – and they are slight!
Pauline Goodwin – Senior Publishing Director, Kogan Page	Confidence in my writing skills when I had none.
Parents	Support, praise and acceptance even when I screw up.

I was going to list an equal number of demotivating people, but I am feeling quite warm and glowy after that one so I am not going to. But do reflect on the demotivators you listed in the 'My way' exercise. Add to the list if you were not precise enough. We must emulate these motivators and expunge any behaviour we have learnt from the demotivator group.

We know from researchers and theorists like Herzberg that there are general circumstances that motivate: achievement,

INSIGHT

There are many reasons why employees become demotivated. The infamous Gerald Ratner, who felt sufficiently at ease to hint that he sold tat, managed to upset shareholders and staff in one fell swoop. Who would want to be associated with a company that doesn't have excellence as its goal even if it is at the bottom end of the market?

By the same token a company may have an excellent product but those managing it may have a less than excellent way of motivating their staff to produce and sell it. An example of this was to be found in a national food production company. The sales manager, Tom, used fear as a motivator. I am sure he really felt this technique worked and in the short term it possibly did. Folk were certainly terrified to attend sales meetings if they had not met their target and a contributory factor was Tom's 'chair' technique he used on defaulters. Once a month, failures had to sit in the hot seat and everyone else in the team had to provide feedback as to their deficiencies. You can imagine wanting to avoid that kind of humiliation with a bit of hard work. But as targets increased, the team just knew that their turn would come for the hot seat. They were so anxious they were desperate to leave. The in-house photocopier was breaking down under the excessive production of CVs. Despite wondering why there is such a high turnover of sales staff, the board has promoted Tom to MD. They talk of Tom as a tough manager and no doubt he is now trying out his motivational technique on the entire company.

recognition, interesting work, responsibility and advancement. But we are also individuals with differing needs and drives. A questionnaire called 'Career drivers survey', which I discovered in *Managing Your Own Career* by D Francis, provides great insight into which of nine major drivers gets us up in the morning. Follow the instructions carefully and see how you fare. I'll talk to you later.

Career drivers survey

A word of warning before you complete this questionnaire. Sometimes you will find yourself struggling to compare two items that appear equally relevant or irrelevant. Please persist. The technique forces you to weigh difficult choices, and the discipline has proved worthwhile.

There are no right or wrong answers – it all depends upon personal preferences, so please be as honest and objective as you can. Work through the questionnaire quite quickly: 10 minutes is usually long enough.

Instructions

Below are listed 36 pairs of responses often given by people when they are asked about what they want and need from their career. You must evaluate the relative importance to you of the statements within each pair and allocate three points – no more, no less. In other words, the possible distribution of points between the two items in the first pair, for example, would be as follows:

Choice one: A = 3 points   B = 0 points
Choice two: A = 2 points   B = 1 point
Choice three: A = 1 point   B = 2 points
Choice four: A = 0 points   B = 3 points

The letters given before each item are for the purposes of scoring and need not concern you at this stage. Just make sure that when you have completed each pair three points have been given each time.

Career drivers survey questionnaire

Score

1. A ... 1   I will only be satisfied with an unusually high standard of living.
   B ... 2   I wish to have considerable influence over other people.

2. C ... 3   I only feel satisfied if the output from my job has real value in itself.
   D ... 0   I want to be an expert in the things I do.

3. E ... 2   I want to use my creative abilities in my work.
   F ...   It is especially important to me that I work with people I like.

4. G ... 1   I would obtain particular satisfaction by being able to choose freely what I want.
   H ... 2   I want to make quite sure that I will be financially secure.

5. I ... 2   I enjoy feeling that people look up to me.
   A ... 1   Not to put too fine a point on it, I want to be wealthy.

6. B ... 2   I want a substantial leadership role.
   C ... 1   I do that which is meaningful to me, even though it may not gain tangible rewards.

7. D ... 1   I want to feel that I have gained a hard-won expertise.
   E ... 2   I want to create things which people associate with me alone.

8. F ... 0   I seek deep social relationships with other people in my work.
   G ... 3   I would get satisfaction from deciding how I spend my time.

9. A ... 1   I will not be content unless I have ample material possessions.
   D ... 2   I want to demonstrate to my own satisfaction that I really know my discipline.

10. C ... 3   My work is part of my search for meaning in life.
    E ... 0   I want the things that I produce to bear my name.

11. A ... 2   I seek to be able to afford anything I want.
    H ... 1   A job with long-term security really appeals to me.

12. B 3   I seek a role which gives me substantial influence over others.

    D 0   I would enjoy being a specialist in my field.

13. C 3   It is important to me that my work makes a positive contribution to the wider community.

    F 0   Close relationships with other people at work are important to me.

14. E 2   I want my personal creativity to be extensively used.

    G 1   I would prefer to be my own master.

15. F 2   Close relationships with other people at work would give me special satisfaction.

    H 1   I want to look ahead in my life and feel confident that I will always be OK.

16. A 2   I want to be able to spend money easily.

    E 1   I want to be genuinely innovative in my work.

17. B 2   Frankly, I want to tell other people what to do.

    F 1   For me, being close to others is the really important thing.

18. C 2   I look upon my career as part of a search for greater meaning in life.

    G 1   I have found that I want to take full responsibility for my own decisions.

19. D 2   I would enjoy a reputation as a real specialist.

    H 1   I would only feel relaxed if I was in a secure career.

20. A 1   I desire the trappings of wealth.

    F 2   I want to get to know new people through my work.

21. B 1   I like to play roles that give me control over how others perform.

    G 2   It is important that I can choose for myself the tasks that I undertake.

22. C 3   I would devote myself to work if I believed that the output would be worthwhile in itself.

    H 0   I would take great comfort from knowing how I will stand on my retirement day.

23. F 2   Close relationships with people at work would make it difficult for me to make a career move.

    I 1   Being recognized as part of the 'establishment' is important to me.

24. B ²... I would enjoy being in charge of people and resources.
    E ¹... I want to create things that no one else has done before.

25. C ²... At the end of the day, I do what I believe is important, not that which simply promotes my career.
    I ¹... I seek public recognition.

26. E ²... I want to do something distinctively different from others.
    H ¹... I usually take the safe option.

27. B ²... I want other people to look to me for leadership.
    I ¹... Social status is an important motivator for me.

28. A ²... A high standard of living attracts me.
    G ¹... I wish to avoid being tightly controlled by a boss at work.

29. E ³... I want my products to have my own name on them.
    I ⁰... I seek formal recognition by others of my achievements.

30. B ³... I prefer to be in charge.
    H ²... I feel concerned when I cannot see a long way ahead in my career.

31. D ²... I would enjoy being a person who had valuable specialist knowledge.
    G ¹... I would get satisfaction from not having to answer to other people.

32. G ⁰... I dislike being a cog in a large wheel.
    I ³... It would give me satisfaction to have a high-status job.

33. A ⁰... I am prepared to do most things for material reward.
    G ³... I see work as a means of enriching my personal development.

34. I ³... I want to have a prestigious position in any organization for which I work.
    H ⁰... A secure future attracts me every time.

35. F ²... When I have congenial social relationships nothing else really matters.
    D ¹... Being able to make an expert contribution would give me particular satisfaction.

36. I ³... I would enjoy the status symbols that come with senior positions.
    D ⁰... I aspire to a high level of specialist competence.

© D Francis, *Managing Your Own Career*, HarperCollins

Scoring the career drivers survey

To score the survey, add up all the points that you have given to each of the A, B, C, D, E, F, G, H and I items. Write the totals in the boxes in Tables 1.1 and 1.2, and check that the grand total is 108. Copy these scores on to the Career Drivers Profile in Table 1.3.

Table 1.1

A	B	C	D	E	F	G	H	I	
9	17	20	8	13	10	10	6	14	

Table 1.2

A	B	C	D	E	F	G	H	I		
+	+	+	+	+	+	+	+	+	=	108

Table 1.3   Your career drivers profile

Mark your scores on the chart below by circling the numbers you scored for each letter. Then join up the circles to give a diagrammatic profile of your personal career drivers. When you have done this, read the next section to interpret your profile.

24	24	24	24	24	24	24	24	24
23	23	23	23	23	23	23	23	23
22	22	22	22	22	22	22	22	22
21	21	21	21	21	21	21	21	21
20	20	20	20	20	20	20	20	20
19	19	19	19	19	19	19	19	19
18	18	18	18	18	18	18	18	18
17	17	17	17	17	17	17	17	17
16	16	16	16	16	16	16	16	16
15	15	15	15	15	15	15	15	15
14	14	14	14	14	14	14	14	14
13	13	13	13	13	13	13	13	13
12	12	12	12	12	12	12	12	12
11	11	11	11	11	11	11	11	11
10	10	10	10	10	10	10	10	10
9	9	9	9	9	9	9	9	9
8	8	8	8	8	8	8	8	8
7	7	7	7	7	7	7	7	7
6	6	6	6	6	6	6	6	6
5	5	5	5	5	5	5	5	5
4	4	4	4	4	4	4	4	4
3	3	3	3	3	3	3	3	3
2	2	2	2	2	2	2	2	2
1	1	1	1	1	1	1	1	1
0	0	0	0	0	0	0	0	0
A	B	C	D	E	F	G	H	I

A	Material Rewards	B Power/Influence
C	Search for meaning	D Expertise
E	Creativity	F Affiliation
G	Autonomy	H Security
I	Status	

What drives me?

The nine career drivers are:

1. Material rewards   Seeking possessions, wealth and a high standard of living.
2. Power/influence   Seeking to be in control of people and resources.
3. Search for meaning Seeking to do things that are believed to be valuable for their own sake.
4. Expertise   Seeking a high level of accomplishment in a specialized field.
5. Creativity   Seeking to innovate and be identified with original output.
6. Affiliation   Seeking nourishing relationships with others at work.
7. Autonomy   Seeking to be independent and able to make key decisions for oneself.
8. Security   Seeking a solid and predictable future.
9. Status   Seeking to be recognized and admired.

Remember to check your score is 108. Use of the grid alerts you to missed answers. Now look at your profile and circle your top two or three highest scores. These are your main drivers, the sources of energy and direction that shape your life. If we are unaware of these career drivers the danger is that we seek a job or promotion because it is the next step or everyone expects it of us. If a job does not satisfy our major drivers we become dispirited, apathetic, even depressed. Certainly the opposite of motivated.

Here is a list of things to look out for and ways to interpret your scores:

1. The most important question to ask yourself is – does your current position satisfy all of your main drivers? If not, then you must change your role immediately or as soon as is humanly possible. I know this is not as easy as it sounds. Mortgages and rents must be paid. But there are often areas within jobs that you could volunteer for, or you could

delegate the draggy bits to someone who would be motivated by them. (Give 'Career drivers' to everyone in your department or team.) You can then concentrate on the parts that satisfy you.

Alternatively, keep the CV perked up and distribute it to a few agencies or headhunters. It is always good to know your value in the marketplace and this is a strategy used by fast-track managers to negotiate their way to the top. You do not have to leave. It just gives you increased confidence to negotiate. On the other hand this questionnaire may have confirmed your desire for new challenges. If so, then you can use the knowledge of your drivers to interview the interviewer. For example, people driven by high power and influence must ask to whom they will be reporting and if they will be given a free hand to carry out any improvements. High meaning scorers must ask about their level of involvement in decision making, how they will know what is going on and where their job fits into the overall picture. Those of you who have a drive to be experts should enquire about the availability of training and coaching before even considering a position. And so on.

2. Your top drivers will change over time. For example, when I was keen to leave the NHS to set up my own practice, my highest scores by far were power and influence and autonomy. This pattern, by the way, is indicative of entrepreneurial zeal. It may be coupled with a high money score but that is less predictive than the other two. Plan to do your own thing if this pattern is yours.

    As soon as I had set up my own company with another psychologist, Averil Leimon, my drivers changed. Creativity became higher as I wanted to do things differently and affiliation increased as I sought to surround myself with like-minded people.

    Now my creativity score is high as I constantly strive for new ways to coach and train, but a higher meaning score has crept in which was never there before and which surprised me. I think it comes from a desire to make a real difference for clients to engage in meaningful work.

3. Look out for conflict between your scores. If you have a high autonomy and security score then it could be that you are sticking with the wrong job because it is steady. Maybe you are working for a charity and have a high money score. Wrong place for you to be!

Conflicts can obviously be resolved by changing jobs or can be compensated for in your social life. Rose Canning, a shop floor worker in Northern Telecom and a high power and influence scorer, would have been horrified at the suggestion that she should move to a better job. The way Rose influenced was to raise money for charity. She was so good at this that she was awarded an MBE. Life is often about such compromises.

4. Of course if we are leaders or supervisors we must understand others' motivation as well as our own if we want to influence and inspire. The fatal error we commit is to imagine that other people are motivated in the same way as we are. If we look at the drivers list on page 36, we can start to imagine what other people's drivers are and how we can so easily demotivate if we do not take this information into consideration.

■ A high *meaning* scorer needs you to spend time with them so they understand what is going on. They are easily demotivated if you are too busy to meet them or cancel appointments, even for the best of reasons.

■ We may have noticed a head of department or team leader was overworked and suggested splitting the role to help ease the pressure. The high *power/influencer* will be so insulted as you have just eroded their power base, even if it were for the best possible reasons. You would need to find a way of making this person in overall charge while bringing someone else on board to help.

■ High *material rewards* scorers can be demotivated by a delayed paycheque or a late or lesser bonus.

■ Bringing another *expert* in to provide a boost for a department may seem a great idea, but what will the resident expert feel? This must be handled with care.

■ The worst thing you can say to a high *creativity* scorer is just do it the way we have always done it. Boredom will ensue.

■ To suggest to people with a high *affiliation* drive that they should work on their own will have them looking at the appointments pages before you put a full stop at the end of your sentence.

■ Asking people who are high in *autonomy* to report directly to you so that you can oversee their project and steer it in the right direction, may seem sensible but will profoundly irritate them.

■ Put everyone on short-term contracts and the high *security* scorers will have sleepless nights.

■ Promoting someone without giving them the title or any outward trappings will have the high *status* scorer digging for freedom.

Herzberg and Maslow, the famous motivation theorists, talk of the generalities of what motivates. Herzberg's 'satisfiers' involve responsibility, recognition, opportunity for advancement and work that is interesting. Maslow puts forward a hierarchical process of motivation, in which it is useless to offer advancement or self-development to someone who does not have enough money to pay the rent.

Rewards

Research at a US university into reward was recently quoted by Roger Firestein at the Creative Problem Solving Institute in the USA. Researchers discovered that for students to maintain current performance, tutors had to reward them four times as much as they criticized. But, to improve the students' performance incrementally, tutors had to reward them eight times as much as they criticized. For me this emphasizes the profound effect of reward. There are some important rules to make your rewards even more rewarding.

Rules for rewards

Learning theory research provides the following principles for rewards. They must be:

- *Intermittent.* Rewards are most rewarding when they are not predictable or institutionalized, like pay rises or bonuses. A thank you, a card, a box of chocolates on completion of an assignment, is much more compelling. A parallel is gambling. If you were rewarded with a win every time you bet on something, there would be no excitement and of course no addiction.
- *Specific.* Rewards should be 'for' something well done or that you would like to happen again. To be truly reinforcing you should outline the behaviour you admired like working late three nights in a row or cooking, cleaning *and* washing up, rather than just being nice. 'Nice' is difficult to achieve again if you don't know specifically what you did.
- *Contingent.* A 'thank you' of any sort is more powerful if it is given immediately after an event rather than a week later, at the end of the month or at the end of the year. We associate the good feelings that accompany the reward with the action that led to it and are more likely to act that way again or even better next time. A Managing Director I work with, Iain Kennedy (one of my motivators), phones me as soon as I have completed a training course for his staff to give me any positive feedback he has received. The effect it has is for me to want to work harder, longer and more effectively to achieve that reward.
- *Consistent.* If you reward one person for going that extra mile, you must notice and celebrate other extra miles. Unfairness ruins the entire process and leads to accusations of favouritism.
- *Relevant.* Tap into your knowledge of the career drivers of your team or department to choose a reward that suits and will motivate. There is the cautionary tale of the MD of a shipping company. The organization had gone through tough times during the recession but had recovered through the good services of the staff, who had put in extra

hours and taken pay cuts. The MD had dreamt of rewarding the entire workforce and their families with a Christmas cruise to celebrate the turnaround. But as he jauntily put up the poster advertising the event, the workforce went on strike. He was devastated. Can you guess the reason? He hadn't asked them what *they* would like to do. It had been his dream, not theirs. They would have preferred a less expensive party and some money for presents for their kids who had been deprived of luxuries during the recession.

■ *Genuine.* Flattery for the purpose of ingratiation or achievement can be easily spotted (especially in the tone of voice and body language). Rewards and compliments must be genuinely felt and sincerely praised.

Celebrate winning

One last exercise for this chapter: write down at least six ideas to celebrate winning. Half of them should be personal rewards, rewarding yourself for an achievement or completion of a project. If you work in a team, write down things you can do together to mark success. NB: These must be ideas you have never used before.

Life is so hectic that we have barely finished one project before embarking on another. Closure and the reinforcement of success are so important and raise morale.

Celebrate winning

Note your ideas here to celebrate winning (only new ideas please).

■

■

■

■

■

■

INSIGHT

Julian Richer, the very successful owner of Richer Sounds, puts reward at the top of his leadership skills list. He owns 11 houses; two he lives in, but the other nine he makes available for his staff. Good performance by any employees is recognized with a holiday in one of his homes.

A last thought

I visited an art exhibition in Glasgow's George Square where exhibits from all the major galleries in Britain were present. The standard was universally superb, but one piece caught my eye. It was a square of glass engraved with the following:

> WITHOUT
> KNOWING WE
> LEAVE A
> TRACE OF OUR
> SELVES

It set me pondering about what we leave behind. Are people enriched by our presence or depressed by it? And since others mostly just see our body language as we go about our business, could it do with being more exuberant, more expressive, more giving?

Of course I had to buy that glass for my office and there it hangs on my wall to act as both inspiration and reminder.

Step 1 checklist

1. First impressions are important if we want to progress. If you do not desire promotion, progression or any other 'p' you can think of, then disregard all ensuing advice.

2. Be positive about your attributes and find a way to sell what you do in a captivating way.
3. Change your body language to include open gestures, eye contact and smiling if you want to endear yourself to others. Remember Peter's strategies.
4. Become more sensitive to others by indulging in body language sleuthing. Pick up on what others are doing and intervene where necessary. Ask questions or mirror, pace and lead.
5. Become an expert in what motivates you in your career. Be prepared to use that information to ask questions at interview about what will continuously motivate you.
6. Understand others' drivers because they will more than likely differ from your own. Learn to reinforce these drivers at every opportunity.
7. Reward the people around you eight times more than you criticize them if you want them to improve.
8. Celebrate winning at every opportunity and have fun in everything you undertake, especially at work.

Key learning points

Now rerun the chapter and list, in Table 1.4, as specifically as possible, all the points that you wish to remember to put into practice.

Table 1.4   Key learning points

Key learning points that I found particularly useful from Chapter 1	How I intend to put these into practice
1. ⟶	
2. ⟶	
3. ⟶	
4. ⟶	
5. ⟶	

Step 2

Thought

How to develop a variety of thinking styles

Faulty thinking

There is a story of a man who thought he was dead. He visited his doctor and said 'I think I am dead.' His doctor worried about his mental state and put him on Prozac. Two months later he was back at the surgery. 'I think I'm dead', he said again. This time he was sent to a psychiatrist. Two months later there he was again saying 'I think I'm dead.' Suddenly the doctor had a brilliant idea. 'Dead men don't bleed do they?' the doctor exclaimed to his patient, who agreed with him. So he seized a knife and made an incision in the patient's hand from which blood gushed. 'Oh my God,' said the man, 'dead men do bleed.'

Our thoughts are not at all easy to change, especially if we have had them for a long time.

Aaron Beck, a famous cognitive therapist, back in the days when he was using psychoanalytic techniques, discovered during free association (sessions where patients are asked to talk about anything that comes into their heads) the existence of what he called 'automatic thinking'. Here he tells of his discovery. This extract is from *Cognitive Therapy and the Emotional Disorders*.

These automatic thoughts reported by numerous patients had a number of characteristics in common. They generally were not vague and unformulated, but were specific and discrete. They occurred in a kind of shorthand; that is only the essential words in a sentence seemed to occur – as in a telegraphic style. Moreover, these thoughts did not arise as a result of deliberation, reasoning or reflection about an event or topic. There was no logical sequence of steps such as in goal-orientated thinking or problem solving. The thoughts 'just happened' as if by reflex. They seemed to be relatively autonomous, in that the patient made no effort to initiate them and, especially in the more disturbed cases, they were difficult to 'turn off'. In view of their involuntary quality they could just as well have been labelled 'autonomous thoughts' as automatic thoughts.

In addition, the patient tended to regard these automatic thoughts as plausible or reasonable, although they may have seemed far-fetched to somebody else. The patients accepted their validity without question and without testing out their reality or logic. Of course, many of these thoughts were realistic, but the patient often tended to believe the unrealistic thoughts, even though he had decided during previous discussions that they were invalid. When he took time out to reflect on their validity or discussed their validity with me, he would conclude they were invalid. Yet, the next time that he had the same automatic thought, he would tend to accept it at face value.

The automatic thoughts Beck describes are a kind of inner dialogue that continues in our heads even as we are talking about something completely different. This dialogue can propel us to great things or talk us out of new situations and challenges. Although not easy to change, changed it can be. And as soon as you embark on step two of this makeover you will feel and act in a much more energetic and purposeful way.

The wrong labels

Let's begin to tap into *your* thoughts and thinking styles. Be as honest as possible and complete the following exercise.

The labelling exercise

I would like you to make a list of five words, phrases or traits that describe you best:

1. As you see yourself.
2. The view of a superior at work.
3. The view of a relative or partner.

Give yourself about five minutes to complete this exercise. Do not deliberate too long, as first thoughts are best.

1. As you see yourself.

I am . . . .

I am . . . .

I am . . . .

I am . . . .

I am . . . .

2. The view of a superior at work.

I am . . . .

I am . . . .

I am . . . .

I am . . . .

I am . . . .

3. The view of a relative or partner

I am . . . .

I am . . . .

I am . . . .

I am . . . .

I am . . . .

When you have filled in all the spaces, I would like you to judge whether your words, phrases or traits are positive or negative for each of the sections and place a plus or minus sign where relevant.

Reflect on the following questions:

■ Did you have more positives than negatives overall?
■ Did negatives cluster in one section more than the other two?
■ If you do have some negatives, why did you not consider a list of 15 positives? And if you did consider it, what stopped you?

This exercise strikes at the heart of self-esteem. If you have written 15 positive statements, well done. For those of you with some negatives, the interesting fact is that I am sure if I met you I could come up with 15 or more positive traits to describe you. So what stops our own positive self-appraisal? Humility? Upbringing? Culture? Perhaps a cocktail of all three.

Of course, we have weaknesses, but we all too often emphasize those at the expense of our strengths. And sometimes these perceived weaknesses have outgrown their usefulness and we have advanced in skills and confidence way beyond that label. It's as if inside us what we believe about ourselves is slow to catch up with external reality. We have had these thoughts for so long that they automatically come to mind when we think about ourselves – the kind of thoughts Aaron Beck talked about. Labels that are wrong are one example of faulty thinking.

As I am writing this, I am remembering a young women called Donna who, during the labelling exercise on a confidence-building programme, had written that she saw herself as 'quiet' and a 'failure'. Her friends in the group were horrified by this description of someone so lively and attractive. She told us that she came from a large Italian family and, yes, she was a little quieter than the rest. As a result her mother would introduce her as 'Little Donna, the quiet member of the family'. To us, she was positively ebullient but perhaps a trifle more subdued in the arm-waving department compared to other Italians we had met. 'But so what!' we said with one accord. It was great feedback for her and encouraged her to tell the rest of her story.

Her ambition as a child was to get into the top stream when she went to secondary school. She missed it by a couple of marks in the exam but was encouraged to try again the following year. She did, but again missed by a few marks. A teacher took her aside and told her that it was better to be a big fish in a small pond than a small fish in a big pond. From that day, she remembers, she stopped trying. More horror from the group who had always seen her as a successful sales person.

That evening, she tells me, she changed her view of herself. She returned home to a husband who was unemployed but did nothing around the house nor helped with the children. Despite her positive support of him, he was often verbally and physically abusive. That night she thought 'I'm better than this.' By the end of the month she had moved to a small cramped bedsit with the children. She went for interviews for better jobs and eventually bought her own flat. The last I heard she had met a charming, successful man who thought she was just wonderful and had proposed to her.

A story rarely does justice to the struggles and hardship along the way, so the denouement can seem trite, but believe me Donna's success started from the moment she changed those labels. Do you have any worn out, way past their sell-by date labels? Check with friends and relatives. Reminisce as to their genesis. Then if they no longer hold water, throw them out.

INSIGHT

David Schwartz, in his book *The Magic of Thinking Big*, talks of how we use labels as excuses for inaction. We are too tall, too short, too fat, too thin, too lively, too quiet, too anything to be successful. He advises getting rid of the labels, get rid of the excuses and dare to think big.

Sometimes, feedback from your nearest and dearest may reinforce some of your weaknesses and add a few more. If so, write the opposite beside the negative statement and make that a goal for change, if you want to change of course. I say that advisedly as there may be some negative aspects you don't want to change. Let me give you an example.

I am particularly undomesticated. Dusting and hoovering seem such a waste of time to me when the dust just comes back again. The last thing I want to do is change that, because there are so many other things I want to do. But there are other weaknesses, like not filing my own personal stuff for three months, not clearing my desk so that an old sandwich could be happily hibernating under the clutter, and wanting everything in my life to happen instantly. These things I am struggling to change even as we speak. (In fact, I have just noticed that I have a black leather blotter thing on my desk, so my filing programme must be working.) Plan to change the aspects you want to change or just forget these weaknesses and glorify your strengths.

In this chapter we will discuss a number of different ways of thinking, not just an adjuration to think more positively, as I have always thought that so insulting. Your partner has just left home, leaving you with all the debts including mortgage arrears, the project you are working on has moved its deadline forward to the end of the week and your best friend has just been taken into hospital with a suspected tumour. If someone who's just been on a positive mental attitude course says to you 'Hey, think positively, things could get worse', they would probably get a justified mouthful of abuse. We are sophisticated enough now to know that different thinking styles are needed for different situations.

INSIGHT

A regional council in Scotland took the bold step of bringing in a consultant who promised to convert staff attitudes from cynicism to a more positive state of mind. Sadly, despite the consultant's best efforts, the whole process entrenched and polarized beliefs rather than the reverse. After the series of seminars, converts would chastise non-believers during meetings if anyone dared to criticize a process or a person. 'Think positively', they would shout with a kind of missionary zeal more characteristic of an American Southern Baptist, to be greeted by the grinding teeth of the opposition.

The skills taught were too simplistic. Of course there are crises, problems and difficult people. To pretend that everything is wonderful when palpably it is not is to indulge in unreality and dissembling.

There is a plethora of thinking styles to meet challenges of all sorts and positive thinking is just one of them. I am trying to think of an analogy. When penicillin was first discovered there was just one form of the drug. Now there are many derivatives to suit all sorts of ailments and to avoid all types of side-effects. Thinking also has moved on.

Assessment of problems

First, let's identify any issues or problems you have. Tackle the 'Sentence-completion assessment of problems' below. This checklist is not intended to depress you but to help you discover solutions and perhaps change your thinking as you proceed through this chapter. Again, try to work speedily. If some answers elude you, move on to the next. But do try to complete as many as possible.

Sentence-completion assessment of problems

1. My biggest problem is…
2. I'm quite concerned about…
3. Something I do that gives me trouble is…
4. Something I fail to do that gets me into trouble is…
5. A social setting I find most troublesome is…
6. The most frequent negative feelings in my life are…
7. These negative feelings take place when…
8. The person I have most trouble with is…
9. What I find most troublesome in this relationship is…
10. Life would be better if…
11. I don't cope very well with…
12. What sets me most on edge is…
13. I get anxious when…
14. A value I fail to put into practice is…
15. I'm afraid to…
16. I wish I…
17. I wish I didn't…
18. What others dislike most about me is…
19. What I don't seem to handle well is…
20. I don't seem to have the skills I need in order to…
21. A problem that keeps coming back is…
22. If I could change just one thing in myself it would be…

Now let's look at the nature of faulty thinking to see if it applies to you and then explore ideas to change it.

First, you have to remember that this thinking is automatic. It just seems to come out of nowhere and flash into our minds without us even being aware of its existence. It may seem very plausible at the time and because it is part of you, like breathing, you accept it as perfectly reasonable without questioning. But if challenged with facts you begin to realize just how illogical it is.

Next you need to discover what kind of faulty thinking you indulge in. We have already talked about wrong labels in the labelling exercise, but it is worth adding that the words we use to describe situations, others and ourselves have an important impact. For example if I say 'I am in a complete panic' or, 'I am totally useless', this dramatic language triggers an anxiety response and literally changes the biochemistry of the body. If we analyse these statements rationally on a scale of 1 to 10 it is doubtful whether we would be at the extreme 10 end of the spectrum of either life-threatening terror or a state of utter immobility. To change this style of thinking, it is important to describe feelings and reactions accurately since this helps to maintain control in a situation.

I was severely put to the test when I was asked to speak at a conference in Brighton a few weeks ago. I managed, goodness knows how, to get on the wrong train, which stopped at Horsham and went no further. This was some 30 miles from where I should have been meeting the organizers at that moment. There is something about railways and railway officials that brings out the worst in me and so I found myself telling the nearest blue uniform that this was a complete disaster which was entirely his fault. Mid-fulmination some memory of coaching others in similar plights, some vestige of learnt behaviour, returned and I realized that the more I carried on like this the less time I had for problem solving. And on a scale of 1 to 10 how disastrous was this really? It possibly hit a 4. So I got myself out of the station and persuaded the taxi queue that my need was greater than theirs and £50 lighter and 40 minutes later I was at Sussex University speaking to the group just three minutes after the start time.

Quick hints

Here are some quick hints for overcoming wrong labels.
You need to:

- Catch yourself using words like 'awful', 'dreadful',
  'disastrous'.
- Ask yourself – how awful is this really?
- Problem solve. Once you have relaxed a little, finding
  solutions and becoming creative are so much easier.
- Using a scale of 1 to 10 helps to clarify. Your situation
  is usually less than a 5 unless you are being held up
  by an armed assassin with a balaclava and sawn-off
  shotgun. Then you're allowed a 10.

Exaggerating or 'catastrophizing'

Exaggerating or catastrophizing is certainly my favourite
thinking style in any form of setback or crisis. I don't do it on
purpose, of course, but thoughts of disaster come unbidden to
my mind. I can make any hillock into the Himalayas in a nano-
second. This trait I can trace directly to my mother. We both
have this thing about purses. They are never misplaced – they
have been stolen. In my case, someone has outwitted the door
call system which includes security cameras and locking
devices, broken into my flat, found my purse when I never can
and escaped undetected. The irrationality of this argument
doesn't stop the continuation of these thoughts and I have to
work terribly hard to contain them.

In times of stress and change at home and at work these
thoughts proliferate. Coffee rooms in businesses and offices
must teem with exaggerated predictions of personal disaster as
soon as the word 'reorganization' is mentioned. The fact that
nothing, no matter how bad things get, comes near to these
prognostications doesn't stop us indulging in such thoughts

again and again. So why do we do it? Do we really believe it is the end of the world as we know it?

Part of the explanation for me is that if I think the worst it might not happen. A kind of superstitious thinking. The trouble is though that I get so agitated that the chances of finding my purse even if it were in front of me become remote. And I stir up people around me needlessly. And while I then recover quickly, they are still upset.

Quick hints

So if, like me, you exaggerate or catastrophize:

- Relax.
- Do nothing, say nothing for 5 to 10 seconds till you have thought the issue through.
- If something is lost, calmly retrace your movements and you will usually remember exactly where you left it. Anxiety interrupts your memory; relaxation restores it.
- Try that rating scale again, or anything to relax you.
- Try saying 'This is not a big deal, I can cope. I have before and I will again'.

Useful thinking

An ability to modify and be in charge of our thinking allows us to react more effectively and appropriately to events in our lives. That is not to say there is no place for unhappiness or upset; there is. But at some stage we are ready to move on, and 'useful thinking' speeds up that process and means that we modify those old automatic thoughts to move us purposefully towards solutions to our problems.

Table 2.1 shows some examples of faulty thinking which use negative language in a situation like a presentation or interview. It also shows 'less effective thinking', which is marginally better as

Table 2.1

FAULTY THINKING	LESS EFFECTIVE THINKING	USEFUL THINKING
I'm so nervous. I've blown it!	Don't get anxious! You'll blow it!	I am usually calm and confident – cope with it.
I was a total failure – everyone will think I'm an idiot.	I wasn't a total failure. Maybe next time.	Most of it was OK. I'll know what to do next time.
I didn't get anything I wanted. I'll never do any better.	I didn't get all I wanted. I should have done it better.	I didn't get everything I wanted, I did it and that's really positive. I'm making progress.

YOUR EXAMPLES

FAULTY THINKING	USEFUL THINKING

you are telling yourself to stop, but the negative language counteracts that advice. Useful thinking, in the third column, is not over the top but talks instead of 'coping', 'success next time' and 'beginning to make progress'. Add examples of your own faulty thoughts, past or present, then change the language to more useful thinking. Note the difference in how these new thoughts can change the way you feel. Don't bother with the less effective thinking column. It's not good to learn the wrong or less effective way of doing things. Go straight for success and mastery.

Add your own examples using a few of the problems you identified in the 'Sentence-completion assessment' exercise. Remember to change your faulty thinking to useful thinking

INSIGHT

Elizabeth, a young, recently qualified architect had been identified by her company as a potential star. This meant that she had to accompany the senior partner to business meetings and present her ideas to clients. Despite being very confident about her professional abilities, she became increasingly reluctant to take part in these client visits. When anyone asked her a question or disputed a figure, she would blush to the roots of her hair. There is no use advising a blusher that it looks attractive or that no one really notices because to him or her it is profoundly uncomfortable. At the end of the day what really had to change was her thinking.

You see she had begun to exaggerate and catastrophize even before the event. 'I bet I'll blush today because there are some really high-powered people attending this meeting. When I blush I will start to stammer and it will look as if I am a fool and I am going to let the company down.' Even if the room were slightly hot, that became sufficient to trigger her blushing response.

What changed Elizabeth was thinking more usefully. One of the main coping strategies she employed was to challenge herself with 'OK, so I blush. It is not the end of the world as we know it. It will pass and I will get back on track. The presentation will be fine.' Another technique – paradoxical intention – also helped. When the room was hot she tried to make herself blush. 'Blush damn it,' she would say to herself. And of course she couldn't.

Gradually she stopped anticipating disaster, she coped with her blushing if it arose, which it did less often, and she was free to become the star she was.

using positive words, not 'I will not be disorganized'. 'I am usually organized and I will be again if I spend a day sorting myself out' is a better example.

All-or-nothing thinking

All-or-nothing thinking is a thinking style I have noticed in friends and clients, and it's the kind of thinking that goes hand-in-hand with perfectionism. It involves seeing the world as black and white, right and wrong and entails a 'nothing's worth doing unless you do it well' philosophy. This all sounds terribly laudable until you see how limiting and stressful it is.

A very bright manager I was coaching was an all-or-nothing thinker. 'You win or you lose. Nothing else is relevant', he would say. Even in everyday conversation around the office he would have to win every argument. He would put people down and actually say 'Are you stupid or something?' to ideas and suggestions not to his liking. The thought that he might make a mistake was alien to him and he had no tolerance of mistakes in others. Actually, he was a very witty, intelligent guy when he relaxed, but the outcome of his thinking and behaviour was that he was roundly hated. Of course, when presented with feedback from his staff he was dumbfounded. He claimed that he wanted to challenge and stimulate a response in his team, but what he actually achieved was a surly silence as no one wished to be humiliated as he 'won' yet another argument.

Life is full of grey areas and mistakes are unimportant. You recover and move on. In fact I think mistakes are rather endearing. This of course may be some idiosyncratic thinking

---

Quick hints

If you are an all-or-nothing thinker, remember:

■ Mistakes are unimportant – recovery is key.
■ Life is rarely black and white but almost always greyish. Practise thinking grey.
■ You can have fun without winning at all costs. Start doing things for the hell of it, not to be the best around.
■ Relax and tolerate ambiguity. It's good for you.

on my part as I am constantly getting things wrong and completely forgetting things. I have often been known to ask an audience where I am in a talk as I've lost the place. Usually someone's been listening. At least, I work on that principle.

Over-generalizing

I was in Belfast several years ago, running courses for Nortel. We arrived at this very section on thinking with one of the groups and we were talking about failure. Kerry, who was in her 30s, and a very talented head of administration, admitted to being a 'disastrous failure' as a cook. In fact she didn't 'do' cooking anymore. This all went back to a first dinner party five years ago when she was first married. Friends had been invited round one evening to sample a giant pizza (her mother's recipe) and drink some wine. The pizza was ready to be served but its exit from the oven proved fatal. It fell, and life being life, it fell face down. She was struck dumb with embarrassment, threw the bits into the dustbin and marched out for a takeaway Chinese. She remembers saying 'I will never have a dinner party again. I will never put myself in that position of ridicule.' And hasn't since.

We proceeded to chat about this incident for a few minutes, with participants making sympathetic noises. Then I saw the difference between Kerry and myself. What I would have done was pick up the pizza off the floor, dust it down (don't worry, although not domesticated myself, I do have a cleaner), grate a bit more cheese on top and serve it as though nothing had happened. When sharing these thoughts with the group, there were whoops of delight as they had been thinking the same thing, but didn't want to say it!

You see, Kerry was a perfectionist and an all-or-nothing thinker, but also displayed another thinking dysfunction – over-generalizing. This is where, given one failure, you imagine you will only have others. Obviously the two thinking styles are linked, because if she had been a cook like me she would have been utterly unaffected by her culinary fiasco.

At one end of the spectrum, over-generalizing can lead to phobias like a fear of flying when one bumpy flight leads to fears of the same happening again. I used to run a 'Fear of flying' course with British Airways some years ago and I remember Robert, a travel agent, who despite an array of free-flight incentives just would not fly because he recalled a difficult landing 15 years previously. And he was convinced it would happen again. Changing his thinking to allow that his next flight might just be OK (or if not he would cope with it) was the turning point for him. Robert then proceeded to fly round the world, sending postcards to my increasingly jealous staff.

At a more everyday level, this thinking style may not be as dramatic as producing phobias but can be just as limiting. Putting yourself forward for promotion and being refused even an interview, auditioning for a principal role in the opera society to end up in the chorus, or writing a novel and being rejected by the publisher – we have all been there. It is humiliating, embarrassing, upsetting. But if you ever find yourself saying 'I'll never try that again', stop to ask if this is due to a reaction to failure or a genuine dislike of the activity.

If you have read any positive thinking books, then you will be familiar with the stories of people like Edison and his faulty light bulb filaments. 'Just 1,000 ways I've discovered for them to go wrong,' he is supposed to have jauntily quipped when confronted with yet another failure. Or Sylvester Stallone's auditioning trek round 100 studios before being given his big break. How did they achieve that equanimity? Did they go through the pain barrier of distress that we experience or did they bounce back like one of these wobbly dolls ready for more failure? The trouble with speaking to the rich and famous about such things or reading about them in magazine features in dentists' waiting rooms is that the pain has been long forgotten or anodized with the balm of success.

I always feel that the contrary story of fleas is more analogous to our lives. Apparently when someone is training fleas they put them in a tank and place a piece of glass over the top to stop them jumping out, for just 24 hours. The fleas leap up to what they believe is freedom and bump their heads on the lid. A couple of shots of this and a tankful of concussed fleas one day later has them never attempting to jump out again. And so, I think we ourselves put lids on our lives by over-generalizing from only one bad experience. We set limits on our progress, more than anyone else in our lives.

Quick hints

What can we do to become an Edison or a Stallone? Here are some hints to help you stop over-generalizing:

- Tell yourself continuously that failure is OK. It may not be pleasant and may even feel profoundly uncomfortable but it does not make you a bad person or even a lesser being – just human.
- Be upset. Don't cover up your disappointment or control your emotions. You get ulcers that way. And don't even do as I have done in the past and pretend you didn't want the job/part/publisher's acceptance of your book in the first place. That is simply dishonest and stops you learning.
- Ask yourself 'Next time, how would I do things differently?' Or ask for advice. The people on the interview/auditioning/publishing panel could be extremely helpful in directing you to where you might improve your skills.
- If it helps, see yourself as a product requiring promotion or marketing, anything that stops you feeling destroyed as a person and increases your objectivity.
- Become a reality thinker.

Reality thinking

What characterizes all the faulty thinking so far described is emotionality and lack of objectivity. It is also very egocentric. It centres like a whirlpool around us, and is entirely selfish. To break into all of that helps to objectify and realistically evaluate these thoughts.

So choose another faulty thought of your own and reality test, like the one below. Again, focus on one of your problems or issues identified in the 'Sentence-completion assessment' earlier in the chapter.

Reality thinking

a. Evidence
- What evidence is there to support your thoughts?
- What evidence is there to contradict them?

b. Alternative interpretations
- How might someone else react in this situation?
- How would you advise someone else in this situation?
- What evidence is there now to support alternatives?

c. Effect
- What is your goal in the problem situation?
- Does the negative interpretation help or hinder achieving the goal?
- What effect would believing an alternative have?

INSIGHT

The senior partner in a sizeable law firm in the City, had a habit of ordering business books for his colleagues. To an outsider this might look like a very encouraging gesture, but to them it was a sign that yet again they were found wanting. James, this senior partner, prided himself on his ability to keep abreast of the latest business thinking and the gurus who thought it. He was often heard to decry the rest of the partnership, calling them idiots for having poor management skills. He was probably right. But his attitude ensured that these books, expensively purchased, were never read. Some were to be found in bins under desks.

I remember asking him how helpful he regarded his thoughts about his colleagues and in what way his attitude moved him towards his goal of management education. He was dumbstruck as he realized how, single-handedly, he had ensured that the partners would remain forever ignorant about management skills and the contents of business books.

He left the firm and started again with a different philosophy.

Ignoring the positive

When in the grip of faulty thinking we tend to ignore the positive. Those of you with teenage children will know just what I mean. They have not kept their room tidy for months, have strewn their dirty clothes around the house, repeatedly come in late, loudly played music you hate and conversed in monosyllables for at least a year, making it difficult to remember the loveable creatures they used to be. Truth to tell they are rarely all bad.

One company director I was training in motivational skills said that he could cope with anyone and anything, but not his son, George. George had all of the above bad habits and the audacity to want to be a musician, not an accountant like his father. I asked this director when he had last said anything positive to his son, and he was horrified to note it had been

years. In fact his son had made some attempts to foster a relationship with his father by inviting him to a concert and had
recently offered to cook supper. All these overtures had been
treated with disdain by a father who had fallen into a negative
mind set about anything his son did.

It is so easy to get into bad habits. At work, because you see
the same people every day, it is particularly difficult to notice if
anyone's behaviour has improved. Your initial negative
perception of them tends to remain the same despite contrary
evidence. When a manager does change for the better after
years of complaints from employees, nobody notices, or even
worse, they undermine the change.

A team leader I was coaching, called Stevie Lord ('Just call me
Lord' he would shout to anyone he met) had received feedback
from his team that he was arrogant, interested only in his own
agenda and ignored his staff until they made a mistake and
then his fury knew no bounds. He seemed surprised by this
feedback, thinking, I presume, that he was loved by all or at
least admired. When the tenth person repeated the message he
reluctantly admitted that he would have to change. After three
days of coaching, he returned to work and for the first time ever
wished everyone a good morning. Did his team clap with a tear
in their collective eye as in the best Hollywood movies when
the prodigal returns? Did they shout 'Well done, that must
have been a tough change to make'? No. They laughed.

These people, who had complained for years about this man
and his tyrannical behaviour, in a matter of minutes managed
to undermine all his good intentions. When he came for a
follow-up session he talked of his profound embarrassment
and shame that he had ever tried to be different and begged me
not to suggest he try again.

Understandably his team wanted to get their own back for
years of being on the receiving end of his bad behaviour.
However, if they had just noticed the positive changes and
rewarded them, the quality of their working lives would have
been transformed. As they had laughed at him, they predicted
that he would be back to normal soon, back to the man they
loved to hate. And what a self-fulfilling prophecy that turned

out to be. Ignoring the positive can have quite devastating effects, often producing an outcome directly opposed to the one desired.

What should have happened was that Stevie Lord should have introduced the new improved version of himself to the staff more gradually and, of course, they should have been briefed to reward the slightest change. I had to learn from his story and spend much more time on a 're-entry programme' for clients.

Quick hints

So, if you ignore the positive:

■ Ask yourself, is this situation all bad or are there some positive aspects that could be worked on?
■ If your sense of humour is based on put-downs and negatives, work hard to find an alternative. It might be clever, but ultimately it upsets and undermines.
■ There are positives in almost any situation, even the most challenging. Often this is only realized in retrospect, but they are there none the less. This is worth remembering in the next crisis.
■ Try some outcome thinking.

Outcome thinking

Carry out the next exercise and see whether you notice a shift in your thinking by the end of it.

If you notice a change between focusing on your problem and exploring outcomes, then you need to indulge in outcome thinking more often.

As one participant on a course said recently, 'It was liberating not to have to think of a complete solution – just the next step.'

Problem frame

Think of a medium problem from the earlier 'Sentence-completion assessment'. Be specific in your problem choice. Do not choose 'difficult people', for example; choose a particular person or situation. We'll discuss it afterwards.

Answer the following questions:

- What is your problem?

- How long have you had it?

- Whose fault is it?

- Who is really to blame?

- What is your worst experience with this problem?

- Why haven't you solved it yet?

Outcomes

Now ask yourself:

- What do you want?

- How will you know when you've got it?

■ What else in your life will improve when you get it?

■ What resources do you already have which can help you achieve this outcome?

■ What is something similar that you did succeed in doing?

■ What is the next step?

Notice how very different your experience is depending on which filter you use, focusing on the problem or the outcome.

What differences did you notice?

■

■

■

■

Others have commented that they felt less grounded by the problem when focusing on outcomes. They knew what they ought to do but couldn't get away from focusing on the issue.

By using outcome thinking when you have a problem or a crisis, you are shifting to a much more positive frame of mind and a more creative way of operating. Also you are increasing the chances of finding solutions and becoming successful. Successful people overcome adversity, not avoid it.

INSIGHT

Anna was a German entrepreneur I have known for a number of years. Her son Gunter very much wanted to follow in his mother's footsteps and run the business. To this end he had been trying to avoid being conscripted into the German army. He had gone through the lexicon of known communicable diseases, had embarked upon the psychological with symptoms of depression and finally at his last call-up had mentioned in desperation some headaches he had been experiencing.

The army took him at his word and sent him for tests and scans. When Anna returned from a trip to Edinburgh visiting us, it was to the news that they had discovered Gunter had a very rare brain tumour. His headaches had been all too real.

Anna wasted no time in despair, although she must have been devastated. She sent the test results round the world for analysis by six surgeons and asked for their comments. All came back with a different diagnosis. She asked them again for their solutions. Some said do nothing, others that nothing could be done. Only one, in the USA, thought that he could operate successfully.

The family flew to the US and Gunter underwent the operation. After it was over the surgeon congratulated the family on their brave decision because this had been the only successful operation of its kind. Every previous case had died. Anna told me that she constantly visualized Gunter as fully recovered and made her decision on that basis. She chose the solution that provided an outcome.

Gunter has recovered and is working in the family business. The army has left him alone.

Negatively predicting the future

A natural progression from faulty thinking is negatively predicting the future. This is especially a characteristic of people who call themselves 'worriers'. They often have the notion 'Once a worrier always a worrier' – which is only true if you do nothing about it. Let me give you an example of worrying which very quickly deteriorated into negatively predicting the future.

Michael, a director of a company whose success was meteoric, turned out, during a coaching session, to be a worrier. He was a charming, dynamic man but when he really cared about something he worried.

All of us when we are in worry mode embark on a series of short negative thoughts that chain together – one leading to another until we reach a final depressing scenario. I have given you an example of his thinking below. As you progress through his train of thought, discover if you have any similar worries that culminate in visions of angst and Armageddon.

Negative predictions

Worries about my daughter

My daughter is 33, not married, chooses wimps with an earring; no match for her; she'll be all alone; she needs a stable relationship, children, family, etc. She'll be a spinster, lose her looks. I'll have to pick up the pieces and it will be so upsetting. I'll never cope.

We discussed his daughter, who seemed to me to be attractive and choosy, though I have never met her. She had a wonderful job (simply because he said she had to do something while waiting for the right man!) which she enjoyed and had a stimulating active life. What was the problem? None, he admitted grudgingly.

So I asked him to change his script. You can see the difference. Which thinking is the more realistic? The latter I think.

Positive predictions

My daughter is 33, attractive, intelligent and particular about whom she chooses to marry. She has a great career and will go on to become even more successful. When the time is right she will meet some wonderful person; if she doesn't she still has a great life. She is healthy and I love her regardless of her marital status; she will be fine.

After the session he confided that he thought that his worrying might in some way protect and help his daughter, but what he now realized was that none of his family talked to him about issues in case he became upset and worried. He was becoming increasingly isolated within his family.

When we embarked on changing Michael's faulty thinking he was adamant it had not affected his working life, but more probing revealed that it had. He was the catalyst behind the introduction of coaching and training in his organization. He feared that the managing director would not enjoy his coaching sessions because he was quite an aggressive man with the concentration span of a gnat. An example of his thinking about this is outlined below.

Negative predictions

Worries about the MD and training

He might not enjoy his coaching experience; as a chauvinist he may not like his female consultant; he may be bored; he hates being bored; he may reject the experience; and then reject coaching and training for the rest of the company, and then the company won't grow or develop. I will be so disappointed and upset, I will have to leave the company as I suggested the training and the consultants.

Positive predictions

I'm sure he will love his coaching sessions. A consultant hanging on his every word for three days providing development just for him – how could he not enjoy this? He will then wish the rest of the company to be trained in the same way. The place will be better managed, there will be a greater team spirit; productivity will increase in each department and profits will soar. I will be part of this success.

Quick hints

Here are some ways to stop negatively predicting the future:

- Identify your hot buttons – switches activated by words and phrases that start you on the path of visualizing depressing outcomes.
- Stop these automatic thoughts as far up the chain as possible.
- Replace them with alternative thoughts using reality thinking with coping language.
- Follow this thinking chain till a more positive prediction of the future comes to mind.
- Visualize success.

Visualizing success

Visualization is a much more powerful tool than most of us realize. If we visualize a successful outcome, then it is much more likely to happen as we are drawn to that conclusion. It is a kind of mental programming.

The power of imagination is described in Jack Black's book, *Mind Store*, in which he recounts a story:

> I remember I had been moved by the story of a Vietnam prisoner of war who apparently 'played' (in the privacy of his imagination) every single shot of a full 18-hole round of golf every day during his horrendous captivity. He would play each make-believe round from different angles and positions. He would take hours and this allowed him to preserve his sanity while all around him the madness and deprivation of war raged on.
>
> On returning home to the US many years later he eventually got back to his golf club and played his first real round in six or seven years. To everyone's amazement he played the round on level par – better than he had ever done before. He of course was not surprised, since in the confines of a tiny and crude cell he had learnt the importance of controlled imagination.

Sadly the opposite is also true. If we visualize a negative outcome, then it is also more likely to happen. This is not a simplistic 'alternative' philosophy but a quite complex chaining of beliefs and events that culminates in a kind of self-fulfilling prophecy. An example will help.

A number of years ago a patient was referred to me who was obsessed with the notion that her husband was having an affair. She had been embroiled romantically with him while he was married, and he had left his first wife to live with and later marry her. Perhaps she felt if he could do it once, he could do it again. Whatever the origins she constantly looked for signs of his faithlessness. She ruthlessly scoured the telephone bill, phoning unusual numbers; she examined shirt collars for lipstick; she followed him in her car to appointments. Despite being confounded by evidence of his fidelity she would still accuse him of betraying her.

Initially he was supportive, realizing she was upset and anxious. He then tried to ignore it all, but latterly he began to feel pursued and persecuted. 'I wish I could meet someone calm and trusting', he said wistfully one day when it all overwhelmed him. Her worst fears impacted on her behaviour, making her wary and paranoid and gradually led to her fears being realized.

The trick with visualization is to imagine good outcomes as vividly as possible. Think of your mind's eye as a television screen where you are increasing the colour and brightness controls to gain maximum impact. In a daydreaming moment at a bus stop, coffee break, or journey home, imagine successful solutions or positive possibilities to any issue or problem that you might have. This raises your awareness and alerts you to opportunities. A bit like when you buy a red car and that day you become aware of vast numbers of red cars inhabiting the roads of Britain. Our perceptions are heightened and honed towards our goals and desires.

Visualizing success is just one tool in your armoury to combat negative predictions, but I think it can change your whole style of thinking to be less problem-focused.

Here is an exercise for you. Complete the strengths exercise on page 74 and keep it in a diary or desk drawer. On a bad day, take it out and read it. By number 24 you should be feeling refreshed, positive and ready for action.

Step 2 checklist

1. Become aware of the inner dialogue, the automatic thinking, that inhabits our waking hours.
2. Learn to overcome faulty thinking by using a number of the strategies suggested:

■ Wrong labels – change the negative words to positive goals for personal change. Or concentrate on your strengths and forget the weaknesses.
■ Exaggerating and catastrophizing – how bad is the situation really? Indulge in more useful thinking.
■ All-or-nothing thinking – become a grey thinker and leave behind the black and white. Have fun: trying to be perfect is a pain.
■ Over-generalizing – one failure or mistake is not the slippery slope to disaster, it is just one failure. Learn from it and try again.
■ Indulge in some reality thinking and start to weigh up some of your beliefs objectively. Consider alternatives.

The strengths exercise

1. One thing I like about myself is…
2. One thing others like about me is…
3. One thing I do very well is…
4. A recent problem I've handled very well is…
5. When I'm at my best I…
6. I'm glad that I…
7. Those who know me are glad that I…
8. A compliment that has been paid to me recently is…
9. A value that I try hard to put into practice is…
10. An example of my caring about others is…
11. People can count on me to…
12. They said I did a good job when I…
13. Something I'm handling better this year than last is…
14. One thing that I've overcome is…
15. A good example of my ability to manage my life is…
16. I'm best with people when…
17. One goal I'm presently working towards is…
18. A recent temptation that I managed to overcome was…
19. I pleasantly surprised myself when I…
20. I think that I have the courage to…
21. If I had to say one good thing about myself I'd say that I…
22. One way I successfully control my emotions is…
23. One way in which I am very dependable is…
24. One important thing that I intend to do within two months is…

■ Ignoring the positive – some situations just seem so bad that there are no solutions and no betterment. After the fact, we often do note some good things even if it is only that we survived. Look for these positives at the beginning, not the end.

■ Try some outcome thinking: it will often provide you with the next step.

■ Stop negatively predicting the future. When times are tough it is all too easy to see them not only continuing, but also deteriorating. Rarely does reality match our imagination. Try some visualizing success as an antidote.

3. Think about your strengths more often. You do not have to be the world's greatest. Just good.

Key learning points

Now rerun the chapter and list, in Table 2.2, as specifically as possible, all the points that you wish to remember to put into practice.

Table 2.2 Key learning points

Key learning points that I found particularly useful from Chapter 2	How I intend to put these into practice
1.	
2.	
3.	
4.	
5.	

Emotion

How to develop your emotional intelligence

When I was working as a psychologist in the NHS, many students were sent to our department as part of their training. They were always stimulating company but one in particular stands out in my mind. Mark was tall, dark and handsome, but unlike many other attractive men he was not in the least vain. If it's not an outmoded word, I would describe him as charming. The secretaries adored him because he would arrive early to have his coffee with them and listen to their gossip. When he left after his three-month placement they threw a leaving party – which is more than they did for many permanent staff. If asked why he received such special treatment, they said that he brought a bit of light into their lives, which is more than could be said for the other men around them at work or at home.

In contrast, there was another psychologist, David, who may well have been an attractive man, but few would have known as he had a fuzz of facial hair covering the majority of his face. Communication was by grunts when you met him and memos when you didn't. Input at meetings was negative and disparaging. So why the difference between these two people? If you were being picky you might say they were both psychologists and so both should have been trained to be interpersonally fabulous. Sadly, professional life is not like that. Parental influences and inappropriate role models abound in the helping professions as in any other walk of life and it is these influences we are going to talk about in this chapter to help you determine where yours have come from and, if you want to change them, what to change them to.

In Step 1 I introduced you to the concept of emotional intelligence and the book of the same name. I talked about gut reaction and how we have these feelings often before a conscious thought enters our heads. But there is so much more to emotional intelligence than that. In fact Daniel Goleman lists what I covered under five domains.

The five domains of emotional intelligence

1. Understanding your own emotions

This is self-awareness, recognizing an emotion as it happens. It seems on the face of it to be so simple, yet I had a friend who was permanently so serene even when her somewhat boorish husband would laugh at her or put her down in front of others. We all thought 'What a saint!' Yet she told me years later that she was not in touch with her feelings. She was brought up never to be angry. Counselling helped and one day, with a lifetime's propulsion of pent-up frustration, she left her husband.

2. Managing your emotions

This is emotional self-control. For example, it is the ability to pick yourself up after setbacks and failures to go on to greater things, rather than spending hours being depressed. There are some people who sincerely feel that they must be lacerated by the world's woes, but the ability to limit that to situations you can do something about is a sign of emotional intelligence. This skill is, of course, intimately tied up with how we think.

3. Motivating yourself

To get up each morning, to move towards the distant goal of a degree or a promotion (or a book!) takes the emotional control of delayed gratification. With anything in life there are highlights and draggy bits. Motivation helps us raise our eyes to the horizon and work through the less exciting times for the goal at the end.

4. Recognizing emotions in others

Commonly known as 'empathy', you need to be self-aware before you can acquire the ability to be sensitive to others. It involves picking up on the subtleties of body language and emotional expression. The boorish husband of my friend had a distinct absence of that ability or he would have been aware of how we felt about him and, goodness knows, might have kept his wife.

5. Handling relationships

This requires handling emotion in others (and yourself) over a long period of time. In the marital relationship, for example, it is so exhilarating to be in love but sustaining it over time is the real test. Popular leaders in business, politics and the services have the ability to inspire devotion and loyalty through superb social skills. They are what Goleman calls 'social stars'. This chapter will begin to ensure your own social stardom.

We covered two of Goleman's five domains in Step 1 when we discussed motivation and body language in others and ourselves. In this chapter we are going to tackle emotion and relationships.

Emotions can be fabulous and thoroughly disruptive, often, confusingly, at one and the same time. In pursuit of a smoothly controlled life, I have wished away both good and bad emotions in the past, ending up married to the wrong person and working in the wrong jobs. You see, I rated intellect above emotion and thought I could make myself do anything I wanted to – a strange kind of positivism. And I was ashamed of the strong emotions I felt, whether they were anger, love, rejection or affection. They were so uncomfortable, I would sit on these feelings till I didn't know I had them.

You may be thinking that a book that purports to be about transforming yourself to achieve greater things at work would be infinitely more hard-nosed than to discuss emotion. But it is the combination of intellect and emotion that helps us make the right decisions, choose the right people and handle conflict successfully.

Years ago, before I was director of a business, I had a girl friend who was the MD of a large hairdressing organization. She said that there was no place for emotion in business. I recall thinking at the time that her statement was more wishful thinking than reality, but today I would go one stage further and say that the workplace is a seething hotbed of emotional intrigue. People might pretend that they don't care, but being given promotion or denied it, being humiliated or praised, engenders feelings to kill for.

How we handle these powerful stimuli may make a difference between success and failure. But first we have to know what feeling we are experiencing before communicating it to others. How often when asked by a superior about our views on a project have we replied that we thought it was 'fine', while harbouring huge doubts as to its viability? There could be many reasons for this silence, but some of the managers I work with are frightened that their comments and criticism about a project are going to come across as negative. And what are feelings and gut reactions when set against statistics and facts? Having a way to express ourselves calmly and constructively is crucial for successful management.

INSIGHT

A friend had just started working as a manager for a company that manufactured equipment for the Ministry of Defence. He noticed large shapes covered in tarpaulins in corners around the factory. One day his inquisitiveness got the better of him and he looked underneath. Attached to a mechanical object was a label saying 'Urgently needed for 1990' – it was 1995. When employees were challenged about this, they said that they had tried to tell managers that they just did not have the expertise to complete the assignment. They were ignored and there the objects probably sit to this day. A bit of listening on the part of management and persistence in speaking up by the staff could have resolved the problem in 1990.

Recognizing emotions in yourself and others

Below there is an exercise called 'Emotional descriptions'. I have used it in the training of counsellors at work, but it will be equally helpful to you. I have given you a couple of examples of my own. It's worth remembering that 'good' emotions can generate some negative feelings, and vice versa. This may be a combination of upbringing and experience, but is perfectly normal and often revealing about past incidents in your life.

Emotional descriptions

If you are to become emotionally intelligent, then you need to be familiar with your own emotional states. After that you can be much more sensitive to others' feelings. A number of emotions are listed below. Describe what you feel when you experience these emotions and describe them as concretely as possible. For example, how does your body react, what happens inside you, what do you feel like doing?

To get you started I have given you a couple of examples from my own life. You do not have to complete the entire list, just the ones you feel uncomfortable with or which have exerted a powerful influence over you.

A list of emotions for you to describe:

1.	Accepted	9.	Loving
2.	Afraid	10.	Satisfied
3.	Angry	11.	Defensive
4.	Anxious	12.	Free
5.	Attracted	13.	Frustrated
6.	Competitive	14.	Guilty
7.	Intimate	15.	Hopeful
8.	Jealous	16.	Inferior

17. Joyful   19. Rejected
18. Lonely   20. Trusting

Example 1
Anger. When I feel angry:

■ I can feel confused.
■ I feel hot and bothered.
■ I feel instantly vindictive.
■ I want to do something about it now, though I know that would be disastrous.
■ I can feel hurt.
■ I can feel rejected.
■ I feel alive.

Example 2
Love. When I love someone:

■ I feel exhilarated.
■ I feel glowing.
■ I can feel confident.
■ I can feel vulnerable.
■ I can feel less in control of my life.
■ I feel giving.

Now write down your choice and your description of your feelings. Once you have described how you feel when you have these emotions, you should have a wider repertoire of words, phrases and statements to describe your own emotional states and to identify emotions in others.

Write your examples here:

Forming close relationships

The last element of Goleman's recipe for emotional intelligence is the forming of close relationships. So this section focuses on how to make the relationships in your life more rewarding. So often we take those around us completely for granted. Countless favours from parents go unnoticed, domestic tasks from partners and children are merely expected and at work colleagues' support can go unrecognized. If you manage a team, if you have anything to do with customers (both internal or external to the company) or if you have to interface with superiors, colleagues or team members, then you need to recognize the input of others and find a way to reward it. Eric Berne would say that this feedback – he calls it 'stroking' – is as essential as breathing itself.

Stroking

Stroking is a concept created by Eric Berne in his 'transactional analysis' theory. Around the time he formulated this theory psychologists were experimenting with animals. He must have been aware of the early behavioural experiments with monkeys, which revealed that if they were reared separately from their mothers, monkeys appeared comforted by a cloth substitute over a wire shape. They would rub up against it and hug it. If this were replaced by the wire 'monkey' without a cloth cover, the monkeys did not touch it and became withdrawn.

The implications for human behaviour are plentiful. We need from birth to be hugged and stroked, not only to provide us with a sense of security and well-being but also to give us an awareness of the boundaries of our bodies. As we grow older, hugs and strokes are confined to intimate relationships, but we still desire metaphorical stroking, socially and at work. Just like the motherless monkey with the wire replacement, if these 'strokes' are absent then behavioural withdrawal or attention-seeking results.

Giving feedback in the workplace to colleagues and staff is essential to help them feel comfortable with what they are doing and/or to help them change. Lack of stroking at a funda-mental level can lead to an uncaring attitude and a 'psycho-pathic' organization.

Negative strokes

Negative strokes are ways of diminishing people. Ignoring or putting down others' ideas or contributions are common examples. Negative strokes are not to be confused with crit-icism, which can be very positive and helpful if delivered in a friendly and self-developing way. Negative strokes discount people. They help to make people feel inadequate. They erode self-confidence and lead to resentment and over-cautious behaviour. Some examples are:

■ keeping people waiting;
■ not consulting or involving people in decisions that affect them;
■ asking for suggestions when you are already clear about your decision;
■ hurrying people up rather than listening to them;
■ closing an issue before everyone feels they've been heard;
■ over-explaining obvious things as if the listener were inca-pable of grasping the problem or the facts;
■ being condescending;
■ refusing to acknowledge someone's expressed feelings;
■ using jargon;
■ name-dropping.

When people discount themselves ('I don't know much about this but...') they have probably been exposed to negative strokes. They no longer feel secure and have stopped being clear, direct and open.

In transactional analysis it is observed that the strokes that work best are often unconditional rather than solely dependent upon someone behaving in the desired way. Unconditional strokes come with no strings attached and are given simply because the person is OK with you, warts and all. The vital thing about strokes is not so much in the giving as in the

INSIGHT

James was a successful entrepreneur who built up an outsourcing company in London. He was staggeringly successful. A colleague and I met him and his board to talk about staff development. James arrived late, interrupted the proceedings, walked about, talked over the presentation and was frankly rude. That was interesting enough, since he had asked us there, but more fascinating still was the equanimity with which this behaviour was received. No one was surprised or ashamed. He must always behave this way. I remember thinking how it must, at some time, limit his success. Some months later I visited a company in New York that had wanted to set up a joint venture with James' organization. They called off discussions because of his untrusting and discounting behaviour.

receiving: it is important to observe whether the stroked person accepts or rejects the strokes. If they are feeling depressed or low in self-esteem, they may reject the strokes by discounting themselves ('It was nothing, really'; 'It didn't take me long'; 'I'm sorry it was incomplete.') If this happens, you may have to work at building up their self-confidence sufficiently to receive the praise.

INSIGHT

I was working with a senior group from a large hotel chain. One of the women was immaculately dressed in a grey suede suit. I complimented her and she just stared at me. I presumed she hadn't heard so I repeated the compliment. She ignored me a second time and turned away. I realized that her concern with her appearance must stem from deep insecurity. Her view of herself did not match the compliment, so she rejected it.

Characteristics of strokes

Strokes are:

■ 'units of recognition' or rewards;
■ the ways we demonstrate our awareness of the existence of another human being;
■ a biological necessity – although the level of stroking needed varies between individuals.

Strokes may be:

■ positive –
   life and growth encouraging,
   inviting the recipients to feel OK about themselves and others;
■ negative –
   life and growth discouraging,
   inviting the recipients to feel other than OK about themselves and/or others.

Strokes may also be:

■ unconditional –
   given for being,
   about something over which we have no control,
   about you as a person;
■ conditional –
   given for doing,
   about something over which we have control,
   about an aspect of our behaviour, such as work performance.

Strokes are given and received via the senses:

■ hearing –
   the things we say to each other,
   the sounds of music, singing,
   tone of voice (angry, friendly, etc);

■ sight –
  facial expression, gesture, posture,
  via painting, ornaments, scenery,
  through written comments (memos, performance
  appraisals, etc);
■ touch –
  shaking hands,
  holding, hitting,
  through textures and temperatures;
■ taste and smell –
  through food and drink,
  perfumes, air fresheners,
  tobacco.

Individuals and organizations develop characteristic patterns of stroking and this more often than not emanates from the top. One chief executive of a distribution company was mercurial of temperament. He indulged in a kind of unconscious games-playing where he would reward you with the beam of his attention one minute then cast you into outer darkness with a comment designed to humiliate the next. Clever staff quickly realized that only good news received approbation so they would massage sales figures and cover up crises. He would then fly into a rage and castigate them for not being direct and honest. Organizations become extensions of their owners and leaders. Awful thought in this case.

To assess the quality of your relationships complete the 'Stroking patterns' exercise below.

Stroking patterns exercise

Choose six people who are significant in your life; three from home and three from work. You may want to select a partner or spouse at home, and at work a boss as well as colleagues.

Giving strokes

1. When did you last give each of your chosen colleagues and family friends a significant stroke (more than a polite greeting)?

2. Was it positive or negative? Did it invite them to feel OK about themselves and others, or was it some form of put down of themselves or others?

3. What prompted it? Work, personal, hobbies, appearance, etc – your preferences or theirs?

Receiving strokes

4. When did you last receive a significant stroke from each of these chosen people?

5. Was it positive or negative?

6. What prompted it?

At the top of each column in Table 3.1 note down the names of six people with whom you have had close contact recently: three at work (one should be a boss) and three at home. Consider when you have given and received strokes.

Table 3.1 Stroking patterns exercise

NAMES						
Note down the last time you gave this person a significant stroke						
Was the stroke positive or negative?						
What prompted it?						
When did you last receive a stroke from them?						
Was that positive or negative?						
What prompted it?						

Stroking patterns review

After you have completed the exercise, consider the following points.

Review your answers and become more aware of the ways in which you give and receive recognition. Consider first your choice of six people. Are they a good selection or have you included only those people you like most? What interactions do you have, or not have, with the colleagues you like least? And have you included your boss as someone you work with? Do you stroke and reward your staff but forget to stroke people in authority? They are human too despite perhaps having more status or being paid more than you.

Next, review your responses in the section 'Giving strokes'. How might you appear to others? How much time is spent in put-downs compared to positives? Note that constructive criticism is a positive stroke – it implies that the person can do better and you care enough about them to let them know how. How varied are your reasons for strokes? Do you range over work and personal matters, or do you only comment on whatever interests you? People who get on well with others target their strokes, making sure that they pay attention to whatever the other person values.

Consider how you receive strokes. Are you getting a reasonable quantity and variety? Do you feel comfortable with your working group? Is there a lot of joking and put-downs so that genuine praise is outlawed? Check also for any tendency to swap strokes, as this can devalue them. Swapping occurs when we automatically return a compliment, such as when we say 'Yours is nice too'. The overall effect is to cancel out the original stroke, leaving both parties feeling vaguely dissatisfied or disappointed. And finally, do you reward being given a stroke by saying thank you and showing sincere appreciation?

Do you stroke more at work or at home and where do you receive the majority of your strokes? Why is this? Where you stroke less you are probably taking people for granted. And if you can't remember when you last gave a stroke to anybody, then you really need a mind makeover.

Edification

Of course stroking does not have to be confined to individuals on their own. You can reward an entire group or team, or an individual in front of a team. If you ever need to get someone else accepted as an expert in their own right so that a client or colleague can cease to rely on you, then reward their skills openly. This is the true nature of delegation. Where it often falls apart is when we are so insecure that we want all the accolades for ourselves and so deny them to others.

It's a bit like being at a conference. You can hardly stand up and tell an audience how wonderful you are and how lucky they are to be benefiting from your expertise. But someone else can. Which is why conferences are chaired and speakers introduced. This process of third-party credibility is called 'edification'. It is so powerful a tool that it can make all the difference between success and failure. Let me give you an example, which in this instance was not about a person but a party. The principles are, however, the same.

I was in the United States on holiday and the hotel held a get-together to encourage us to be sociable at various events. There was an underwhelmed response from our group who looked as if they just wanted to be left alone. Then one woman spoke up. She said that the shrimp feast in particular was a great night out, the shrimp were plentiful and luscious and moreover it was tremendous value for money. Well, there was a small stampede for the booking form that had been all but ignored a minute previously.

Shrimps, colleagues, team members – all can be edified to great effect if you genuinely wish them to be viewed positively by others.

Culture

I mentioned reward in Step 1 as having a great impact on motivation. Make no mistake, if individuals, groups and entire organizations could change negative emotion to positive, then you would have an entirely different culture.

Below I have outlined the difference between a caring and a blaming environment to help you identify which yours is. If it is more to the right than the left, then you may have to start creating your own environment in your team or department with a bit more recognition and a little less cynicism. Folk often blame 'senior management' for the critical atmosphere in their company, and they may well be right as a culture usually is established from the top. However, you can make a difference. Make your team the most motivated and stroked in the company so everyone is asking what your secret is.

Recently I interviewed Sir Ian McAllister, former Chairman and MD of Ford Motor Company (now Chair of Network Rail) for another book I'm writing. He said how he was not naturally a man who suffered fools gladly but that was exactly what he was trying very hard to do at the moment. I've just reread that sentence and it sounds as if he is surrounded by fools. Of course, I don't mean that. He told me he had set himself the task of helping managers at Ford become more participative and he believed the only way to gain success was to reward even the most facile suggestion. It may have been the first idea that someone had

---

The caring–blaming environment

Caring	Blaming
I like people	I find people wanting
I compliment people	I discover faults
I do not judge	I judge constantly
I can only change myself	Other people should do what is expected of them
I allow others to be equals no matter who they are	Few people deserve my respect
I listen to others' ideas	There is a right and a wrong way of looking at things
I allow others to be right	I am invariably right
I assume responsibility for what goes wrong	I blame others for anything that is wrong

INSIGHT

I was invited to speak to some chief executives in Northern Ireland about reward and culture change. I structured the seminar around how rewarding they were as people, how often they stroked their staff and what they did to celebrate winning. At the end I realized that they wanted me to tell them about 'employee of the month' and financial incentive schemes. I apologized, but wanted to emphasize that caring for your staff, saying thank you, rewarding more than criticizing – all of these cost nothing and produce infinitely more effective culture change than any other scheme on the market.

come up with or spoken about, so to criticize, blame or judge would ensure a stony silence next time creativity was called for.

I had just such an experience – the judging, stony silence kind. I had been invited to a think tank that was discussing the televising of the Edinburgh Festival. A new producer was looking for ideas for interviews, theatre critiques and performance highlights. I had put together about 30 ideas and at the beginning of the meeting talked about the first one on my list. It was probably my best, come to think of it. He looked at me in a withering kind of way and said if that was the best I could come up with then we might as well pack up and go home right now. I know I should have asserted myself and told him I had another 29 such gems but I did not. I flushed a bright red and sat in complete silence for the rest of the meeting. The chances were that I had no gems to offer, but if I had, he missed them. Part of a manager's job is to suffer fools and instil wisdom.

Emotional coaching

Instilling wisdom is best carried out through a coaching process. Sporting analogies and sports heroes abound to help managers train their teams to be more proficient. I could never see the applicability myself and was quite delighted to hear

David Gower, the cricketer, say at a dinner recently that he could find no parallels between cricket and business. But since he was paid handsomely to supply motivational speeches at conferences, he was happy to draw as many comparisons as it took.

Coaching, training, making things happen – the whole management bit is made easier with motivated, happy people. However, people have problems and are not always willing and able. The test is how you handle the bad times and turn them into the good. And key to that is how you cope with the variety of emotions that are hurled at you.

Complete the 'Emotional coaching questionnaire' below. Be honest. Answer the questions according to what you actually do at the moment, not what you might aspire to do. Once you are finished then you can analyse the results.

Emotional coaching questionnaire

1. People really have very little to be sad about

   True   False   Don't know

2. I think that anger is OK as long as it's under control

   True   False   Don't know

3. People acting sad are usually just trying to get you to feel sorry for them

   True   False   Don't know

4. If someone gets angry, they should be excluded

   True   False   Don't know

5. When people are acting unhappy, they are real pests

   True   False   Don't know

6. Stress is good for you

   True   False   Don't know

7. When people are unhappy, I am expected to fix the world and make it perfect

   True   False   Don't know

8. I spend time helping staff sort out their stress problems

   True   False   Don't know

9. I really have no time for sadness in my life

   True (False) Don't know

10. Anger is a dangerous state

    True (False) Don't know

11. If you ignore someone's unhappiness it tends to go away and take care of itself

    True   False (Don't know)

12. Everyone has got to have some stress in his or her life

    (True) False   Don't know

13. Anger usually means aggression

    True (False) Don't know

14. Feelings are private and not public

    True (False) Don't know

15. When you notice signs of stress you need to intervene quickly to help

    True (False) Don't know

16. I don't mind dealing with someone's unhappiness as long as it doesn't last too long

    True (False) Don't know

17. Helping staff cope with conflict is one of my managerial roles

    True (False) Don't know

18. I prefer a happy person to someone who is over-emotional

    True (False) Don't know

19. It's all right to show you're stressed

    (True) False   Don't know

20. When someone is unhappy, it's a time to problem solve

    True (False) Don't know

21. I help people get over unhappiness quickly so they can move on to better things

    True (False) Don't know

22. I don't see someone's unhappiness as an opportunity to learn much

    True (False) Don't know

23. I think when people are depressed they have over-emphasized the negative in life

    True   False   Don't know

24. In my view anger is natural, like clearing your throat

    True   False   Don't know

25. When someone is acting angrily, they are very unpleasant

    True   False   Don't know

26. I set limits on people's anger

    True   False   Don't know

27. When someone acts stressed, it's to get attention

    True   False   Don't know

28. Anger is an emotion worth exploring

    True   False   Don't know

29. I try to change people's angry moods into cheerful ones

    True   False   Don't know

30. Getting angry is like blowing off steam, letting go of the pressure

    True   False   Don't know

31. When someone is unhappy, it's a chance to get closer

    True   False   Don't know

32. People really have very little to be stressed about

    True   False   Don't know

33. When someone is unhappy, I try to help him or her explore what is causing it

    True   False   Don't know

34. People get over anxious spells if you leave them alone

    True   False   Don't know

35. The important thing is to find out why someone is unhappy

    True   False   Don't know

36. When people are depressed, I'm worried they have negative personalities

    True   False   Don't know

37. If there's a lesson I've learnt about unhappiness, it's that it's OK to express it

    True   False   Don't know

38. I'm not sure anything can be done to change unhappiness

    True   False   Don't know

39. When someone is unhappy, I'm not quite sure what he or she wants me to do

    True   False   Don't know

40. Stress is such an overused word, people just use it as an excuse

    True   False   Don't know

41. If there's a lesson I have learned about anger, it's that it's OK to express it

    True   False   Don't know

42. When someone is angry, I try to be understanding of his or her mood

    True   False   Don't know

43. When someone is angry, I'm not quite sure what he or she wants me to do

    True   False   Don't know

44. When someone is angry, I want to know what he or she is thinking

    True   False   Don't know

45. When someone is stressed and anxious I just feel he or she is not coping well

    True   False   Don't know

46. When someone is angry, I try to let him or her know I care no matter what

    True   False   Don't know

47. When someone is angry, I try to put myself in his or her shoes

    True   False   Don't know

48. It's important to help the person find out what caused the anger

    True   False   Don't know

Emotional coaching – scoring

■ *Dismissing* – add up the number of times you said TRUE for the following items:

1, 2, 7, 9, 11, 16, 18, 21, 22, 23, 29, 32

■ *Disapproving* – add up the number of times you said TRUE for the following items:

3, 4, 5, 10, 13, 14, 25, 26, 27, 36, 40, 45

■ *Laissez-faire* – add up the number of times you said TRUE for the following items:

6, 12, 19, 24, 30, 34, 37, 38, 39, 41, 43, 46

■ *Emotional coaching* – add up the number of times you said TRUE for the following items:

8, 15, 17, 20, 28, 31, 33, 35, 42, 44, 47, 48

If you responded 'don't know' more than four times in each of the sections, you may want to work at becoming more aware of emotion in yourself and others.

Emotional coaching analysis

Compare your four scores. The higher you scored in any one area, the more you tend to that style of managing.

■ The perfect score would be zero in the dismissing and disapproving categories, with high scores for emotional coaching, and a peppering of scores in the laissez-faire category.
■ To dismiss or disapprove of another's upset or anger is to force the emotion to become subterranean. All sorts of strange behaviours ensue with hidden agendas being pursued at meetings, and scapegoating others for our wrongs. Staff very swiftly determine whether it is wise to be emotionally honest or whether they should simulate inscrutability.
■ High scores in laissez-faire mean that you are happy to have emotion expressed around you, but don't necessarily feel

you have to intervene to understand or sort it. A high score is fine but it should not be your highest. It should be coupled with an equally high, if not higher, emotional coaching score.

■ When emotion is expressed at work it means that people care. They may not express it well and the language used may be aggressive, but where there's emotion there's life. Dealing with these feelings moves you, your group and the organization on.

■ You don't have to become a therapist to be an emotional coach. If the problem is beyond your expertise, you can get advice from a professional. Most emotional coaching starts with the question 'Why?' – Why do you feel that way? Why do you get stressed about deadlines? Why have you been feeling low?

■ Become an emotional coach for *all* emotions expressed, not just those you feel comfortable with. A head of education, when he came to this section, said that he could understand all emotions except depression. He expected anyone to be over his or her depression in three weeks. After that, he felt they were swinging the lead. This awareness was enough to change his coaching expectations and behaviour.

INSIGHT

The managing director visited a development course I was running just at the point where one of the participants called Tim was telling me that all this emotional stuff was a 'load of crap'. He then turned on the managing director and criticized him in a very career-limiting way about his interest in personal development and the money he was wasting. A lesser man would have flinched and certainly placed Tim on the next redundancy list. This one stated that Tim's views were interesting and they should meet to talk.

Twice a week, Tim met with the managing director, first to discuss why he was so angry, then to be coached in his career. Tim went on to become a consultant and a great advocate of development programmes.

Step 3 checklist

1. Daniel Goleman has helped us discover that emotional intelligence is a good thing.
2. Part of emotional intelligence is the ability to express ourselves. Finding words to describe accurately how we feel, even to ourselves, communicates very directly and helps others take us seriously.
3. Stroking is as essential to our lives as breathing. Positive strokes can include criticism. Negative strokes discount others.
4. Revisit your 'Stroking patterns' exercise and start to stroke more of those people at home and work you have taken for granted. Rewarding behaviour changes cultures.
5. Become an emotional coach for all emotions and realize that where there is emotion there is life.

Key learning points

Now rerun the chapter and list, in Table 3.2, as specifically as possible, all the points that you wish to remember to put into practice.

Table 3.2   Key learning points

Key learning points that I found particularly useful from Chapter 3	How I intend to put these into practice
1.	
2.	
3.	
4.	
5.	

Step 4

Action

How to change your behaviour and improve your people skills

This chapter is all about becoming active in changing your behaviour.

All of us can talk a good game, think and feel that we have changed, but, of course, the proof is whether anyone else notices, especially those close to us.

We are going to concentrate on the activity of quickly and effectively forming relationships, while at the same time providing you with a framework for handling difficult people.

FORE – family, occupation, recreation, education

I coined the mnemonic FORE many years ago for a telecommunications company after it was privatized. The managers, poor souls, had not had to sell their wares before, as they had the monopoly on telecommunications. While they knew they had to indulge in PR events, they were reluctant to converse with their customers. A typical event would comprise two groups – clients and their wives at one end of the bar and the executives at the other. I was drafted in to improve their skills and as part of the programme I introduced FORE:

F = family
O = occupation
R = recreation
E = education

Why FORE? Well, where there are not too many immaculate conceptions, everyone has or has had a family. Most people have had one or more occupations, if you are dealing with the business community. Recreation and hobbies, though perhaps a distant memory, are still an easy topic of conversation for all. And finally education. Everyone has to be educated and, without any elitist notions, it is interesting to hear about schooling and subsequent training.

In other words, FORE provides a structure of commonalities that we can use to get to know someone quickly. On a makeover course, I give participants three minutes each to find out information about each other that they didn't know before. It's always amazing to me what can be discovered in that short space of time.

One of the telecommunications managers who had a little snigger about the FORE exercise found out in his three minutes that a colleague with whom he shared a secretary and occasionally an office had won the marathon the previous weekend. He didn't even know he was a runner.

In this fast-paced world we are so task and target driven we forget that it is the people around us who help carry out tasks and reach targets. They are not inanimate objects. We need to know who they are and what makes them tick. That's the job of managing. If colleagues like you, they are much more likely to go to the ends of the earth for you and, let's face it, that's required most weeks!

FORE is just as good for use on the telephone as face to face. I put together a programme called 'Customer bonding' for a drinks exporter. The staff only had a telephone relationship with their customers as they were scattered around the world. The 'getting to know you' aspect of FORE was a new concept for them. They had previously thought that anything not directly related to business or orders was wasting time. Now the whole department are relationship converts. And business is brisk.

Here are some tips for using FORE.

Try to use open-ended and probing questions when FOREing people. You will get to know so much more than with the yes/no answers you often receive with closed questions. This needs some practice as closed questioning is what we indulge in most. If you really want to bond, ask more probing questions like 'That's interesting, tell me more about that'. Once you grasp the open and probing routine you can just relax and listen without wondering what to say next. It is a wonderful if forgotten social skill. Here are some examples of different types of questions:

Closed	Open	Probing
Are?	What?	How?
Do?	Which?	In what way?
Have?	When?	Tell me more.
	Where?	Describe in more detail.
	Who?	For what reasons?
	Why?	

The emotional bank

Sometimes people are, well, boring! If you're at a party, you would simply avoid them. If it is a colleague, you can sit elsewhere at lunch. But if it's the boss or a lucrative customer, avoidance is not an option. A concept devised by my former partner Laurence Clarke confronts this issue. He suggests trying some 'emotional banking'.

1. *Discover interest.* Ask open-ended questions till you find something in common or a topic less boring than the rest.
2. *Build a credit balance.* Reward all interesting facts and topics. Boring people are seldom rewarded, so this can have the amazing effect of helping them become enthusiastic and animated.
3. *Deposit.* You can invest information and self-disclosure in the conversation or move the topic to more interesting territory. For example, if the chosen interest is football, which, if you are like me, has you glazing over in five seconds flat, then you subtly move to the drunken/sexual exploits of its stars (which would certainly be of more interest to me).

Try this out next time you are at dinner with the boss or are travelling for hours with that all-important customer. The question you must ask yourself is were you as bored as usual or did investing some effort into the relationship pass the time more interestingly?

I use this exercise for training purposes. Recently, on a young managers course, I asked the group, who were split into pairs, to bore the other as they had never bored before. They chose a topic the other person would hate, then bored for Britain. The other member of the duo was instructed to use the techniques of emotional banking. I thought my debrief of the session had been clear, but when I read the feedback sheets one young manager had mentioned that this particular exercise had been such a failure because nobody in the group of 25 was one whit bored despite all their best efforts! Little did she know that her criticism was a great validation of the technique.

A friend who is terribly good at this skill was stuck beside a titled business executive throughout a long and boring dinner. Narrowly rejecting the option of getting quietly inebriated he decided to invest a little energy in the conversation. The only topic offering the barest flicker of enthusiasm for my friend was the venetian blind business this man's son had just purchased. So good was his emotional banking (he has never owned or even noticed a venetian blind in his life) that the executive wrote to him the very next day, offering him all sorts of discounts on every available blind. It was the last thing he would have wanted, but he did admit that it had made a potentially boring evening into an amusing if somewhat bizarre exchange.

Having FOREd and banked and bonded, you may need to move on (or get away) sometimes. You may have been the only person to listen to that poor soul in years and they now have you pinned to the wall at the office party, talking in intimate detail about their butterfly collection. The elegant way to extract yourself is to interrupt with a compliment, always genuine of course, look at your watch or a clock, touch the person's arm, and move them slightly by the elbow if you have to, then keep walking. Anything less than this complete set of skills may result in your being held hostage by a butterfly collector all night.

This, of course, is a worst possible scenario. Usually FORE helps you to meet wonderful, exciting people to whom you might just have nodded before. It's also great for long transatlantic flights. I met a man last year who was chairman of some multinational and lived on the shores of Oregon. He wrote at Christmas saying it was his New Year's resolution to take me to his coastal retreat. I never did go, but it was rather flattering to be asked. And on the way to China, I sat next to a woman who was going to study acupuncture for six months in Beijing. She was fascinating and the 17-hour flight flew by.

INSIGHT

Two executives were on holiday. Their wives had gone shopping, so they met for the first time at the poolside. In turn they asked each other about family, occupation, recreation and education. At some point, one turned to the other and enquired whether they had been on a transformation course and were using FORE. They had both attended the same course, but with different companies. They became firm friends and still correspond.

Even in the best of company cultures there are upset and difficult people – often, sadly, to be found clustered at middle management and more senior levels. So that means that if you want to rise to dizzier heights, you will have to handle these people effectively.

A study at Cranfield University reviewed those attributes of Chief Executives that led to their rise to the board of directors. They themselves rated the ability to communicate and influence a wide cross-section of people as well as coping with the upset and angry ones as top of their skills list. So the successful handle these irritating thorns in the flesh with elegance, while we are left gasping for a retort, usually on the way home. What is the secret of their success? Keep reading and I'll tell you.

Handling difficult people

First though, let's take a look at one of your difficult people. Answer the questions in the box below. Think of a situation you did not handle well – something recent, or perhaps something in the past that still rankles. We are talking about the opposite of mastery here.

My experience with a difficult person

Outline the following:

■ What was the problem?

■ Who was involved?

■ What actually happened?

■ What did you want to happen?

Keep your situation with a difficult person in mind as we proceed through this section.

Figure 4.1 shows you an overview of the steps we are going to cover so that you will become a great influencer. These skills are of course not only for use with the difficult and challenging but also for any situation where you have to convince others of your point of view. However, there is nothing like a seemingly insurmountable problem to focus the mind on using skills on purpose. When things go swimmingly well we tend to do what we always do. And where is the learning in that!

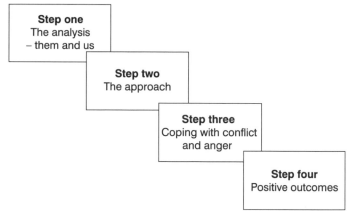

Figure 4.1

One: The analysis – them and us

Before plunging into skills and strategies, you must observe and analyse the behaviour of your protagonist and of course yourself. Here are some questions to prompt your thinking:

■ Is your difficult person difficult with other people too – or is it just you?

■ If some people handle them well, what is it that they do? Observe and learn the skills.

■ What hot buttons do they press in you? In other words, what is it that they do to produce an angry or upset response?

■ How do you respond? Are you sullen in your defiance, sharp with a riposte or do you gaze sphinx-like at them only to retaliate later?

■ Could you be their difficult person? Perish the thought!

INSIGHT

I was working on a company's development programme at one of their outposts abroad. It just so happened that I stayed at the same hotel as the managing director. This helped greatly as we often met over dinner and discussed the progress of the programme. After a few glasses of wine we both became creative, thinking of new ideas and fresh delivery concepts. The next day I would rush in to the training manager, Dennis, enthusiastically expounding what had been discussed at dinner the night before. I wondered why he was always negative and obstructive. One day he told one of the other consultants how much he liked our company, but disliked me. My first response was to dismiss him. My next, on cooler reflection, was to try to see things from his point of view. I had the managing director's ear, something he would have enjoyed. I just expected him to adhere to our enthusiasms, undermining his position. Understanding that I was his difficult person allowed me to begin to repair the damage.

With your powers of observation sharpened, let's progress to analysis.

The analysis – them

Write a list of the irritating and anger-provoking behaviour your difficult person indulges in to make themselves difficult. For example, do they have to be right all the time? Do they never listen to a word you say even after having asked for your advice? Whatever it is they *do* to provoke you, list it below:

■

■

■

■

With the list in front of you, think about what that person wants out of behaving that way. All behaviour is purposeful, so they must want something as a result of the tremendous amount of energy they expend on behaving badly. So, think about their motivation and list what you think they *want* below:

■

■

■

■

You may have listed things like 'They want their own way', or that they desire 'power', 'status', or even 'an easy life'. Whatever you have written, some of these motivations will be quite positive ones. So the motivation may be pure, while the behaviour is not.

The major question that now must be asked is, *Do we ever give our difficult people what they want?* For the most part the answer is no. In fact we often go out of our way to spike their guns and deprive them of their desires. They want attention, we ignore them; if it's power, we undermine them; if they like status, we purposefully erode it. The trouble is, the more we ignore what they want, the more they want it because their needs are not being met. And so the bad behaviour continues.

To be successful in our negotiations we must consider giving them even a little of what they want. This is not as much of a sell-out as it sounds. We are just giving a little to get a little. The story about Mark will elucidate.

Mark was a lovely, earnest guy who had recently been promoted to manage a team of very challenging people in a manufacturing organization. One woman in particular who was the union rep and renowned for her belligerence ran true to form, giving him a hard time during team meetings. She would undermine his every idea, shouting out 'What a load of rubbish' and was an expert dodger of hard work. When we analysed her difficult behaviour we had to use three flipchart pages to capture all her bad habits, then another two to work out what she wanted. He decided that she was desperate for power, status, her own way and probably his job to boot. Then I asked the million-dollar question – 'Do you ever give her what she wants?' He looked shocked at the mere notion of giving her anything at all as he spent most of his time avoiding her. Eventually he agreed to try the approach as an experiment. We worked out that he would give her a project to do at the same time as he was allocating tasks to others, because he didn't want it to look as if he were rewarding her bad behaviour.

He was astonished to find her waiting by his door early the next morning. She had worked through most of the night to finish the project he had set her. She was there to ask for more and to make sure that the rest of the team knew of her endeavours. Mark was amazed – even more so when this change lasted and she went on to become his greatest ally. She later explained that no one had ever given her a chance before, so she became subversive.

The analysis in this process is crucial as it helps you to understand behaviour and motivation so that you can provide the stimulus for change.

The analysis – you

Dr Sue Dellinger has developed a very swift tool to analyse personality characteristics, called 'Psycho-Geometrics'. Complete the exercise on page 114 and suspend judgement till you have made your choices.

Psycho-Geometrics

1. Choose the shape from Figure 4.2 that best describes you.
2. Choose a second shape that also describes you.
3. Look at the 'Quick indicators of shapes' in Table 4.1.

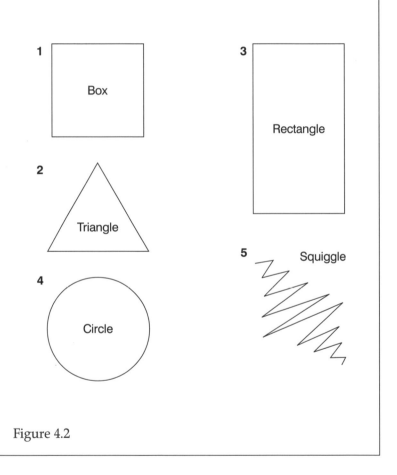

Figure 4.2

Table 4.1 Psycho-Geometrics – quick indicators of shapes

BOX Traits:	TRIANGLE	RECTANGLE	CIRCLE	SQUIGGLE
Organized	Leader	In transition	Friendly	Creative
Detailed	Focused	Exciting	Nurturing	Conceptual
Knowledgeable	Decisive	Searching	Persuasive	Futuristic
Analytical	Ambitious	Inquisitive	Empathic	Intuitive
Determined	Competitive	Growing	Generous	Expressive
Persevering	Bottom line	Courageous	Stabilizing	Motivating
Patient	Athlete		Reflective	Witty/Sexy
Common words:				
Logistics	Interface	Unsure	Lovely	Experiment
Deadlines	Escalate	Consider	'Gut level'	Challenge
Allocate	Jargon	Maybe	Comfort	Create
Policy	Thrust	Delegate	Team	Develop
Efficiency	Return on investment	Options	Cooperate	Conceive
Analysis	'Expletives'	Wait	Feelings	Begin
I did it!	You do it!	Why?	No problem!	What if?
Appearance — men:				
Conservative	Stylish	Erratic	Casual	Sloppy
Short hair	Appropriate	Changeable	No tie	Dramatic
No facial hair	Expensive	Facial hair	Youthful	Dirty
Appearance — women:				
Understated	Tailored	Erratic	Overweight	Varied
Navy, grey	Manicured	Extreme	Feminine	Artistic
Brown	Briefcase	Unusual	Faddish	Fat/Thin
Thin				

Office:				
Every pencil in place	Status symbols	'Mishmash'	Comfortable	Messy
Computer	Awards	Imitator	Homelike	Bleak or
	Powerful	Disorganized	Plants	dramatic

Body Language:				
Stiff	Composed	Clumsy	Relaxed	Animated
Controlled	Jaunty	Nervous	Smiling	Theatrical
Poker face	Piercing eyes	Fleeting eyes	Direct eyes	Mercurial
	Pursed mouth	Giggle	Full laugh	Sexual cues
High-pitched voice	Power voice	High-pitched voice	Mellow voice	Fast talk
Twitches	Mesomorph	Silent	Talkative	Mannerisms
Slow movement	Smooth moves	Jerky moves	Head nods	Fast moves
Precise gesture	Large gesture	Flushed face	Excessive	No touch

Personal habits:				
Perspiration	Interrupts	Attractive	Touching	High energy
Loves routine	Game player	Forgetful	Easy going	Spontaneous
Put in writing	Early arriver	Nervous	Joiner	Disorganized
Always prompt	Joke teller	Late or early	Hobbies	Rebellious
Neat	Power	Outbursts	Sloppy	Works alone
Planner	Handshake	Avoids	Good cook	Life of party
Precise	Fidgety	Variety	Patriotic	Daydreams
Collector	Addictions	Blurts out	TV watcher	Interrupts
Social loner			Socialiser	Fickle

Psycho-Geometrics review

What's this all about, I hear you cry? How can little shapes give you profound psychological insights? According to Susan Dellinger there is 85 per cent concordance between Psycho-Geometrics and other much more expensive and time-consuming psychometric tests. Also it is not so far-fetched when you think that the cars we choose, the houses, the wallpaper, the colours we prefer are all extensions of ourselves. Why not shapes? The results are also uncannily accurate.

- Your second choice acts as a modifier of the first. So if you have chosen, for example, a circle first and a box second, then, although you are very much a people person, you are an organized one. Not for you the distractions of socializing when work is to be done. Your social engagements are likely to be diaried in just the same as other appointments. It is unusual but not impossible for a box also to be a squiggle. Perhaps you have had to modify your creative tendencies for a particular role at work. If you have that combination, then prospective employers ought to know as they will be delighted to have an organized innovator in their midst. I am sure creative people drive the more traditional ones batty with their unrealistic timescales and messy desks.
- You can quickly see why conflicts arise. A squiggle working for a box or vice versa can be in for trouble. They both prize different ways of behaving at work – or at home for that matter. Who cares if your desk is heaped with papers and the occasional old sandwich, when you have just had a brilliant idea? A box, that's who.
- Circles and triangles do not always see eye to eye either. I remember reaching this part of the programme with some offshore medics from an oil company. For two years they had been trying to institute an Employee Assistance Programme and their proposals had all fallen on deaf ears. Eventually they had succeeded mainly because every other oil company had one. Suddenly they realized that as circles they had been extolling the virtues of the programme in humanitarian terms to those with access to the purse strings, who were all, of course, triangles and boxes. They wanted to know the bottom-line difference such an intervention could make, and had not been provided with these statistics. Triangles can be irritated by a circle's perceived softness and woolliness.

- Rectangles always fascinate me because without fail they seem to be people who are in a state of flux in their lives. The other descriptions hardly matter as the overwhelming attribute is a state of indecision and excitement as options are considered and paths explored.
- For a team to operate successfully, different talents and types of people are needed. Can you imagine an entire team of circles? Great fun, lots of cups of tea but few targets reached. It is a case of *vive la difference* for effective teamwork. This has to be accompanied by understanding others around you. If you understand, then you can forgive and respect.

INSIGHT

A journalist interviewed me recently. She had read an article in *Interiors Magazine* about the choice of interior design and different personality types. She wished to improve on this concept and asked me to provide more detail. I was casting about for a framework when I remembered Psycho-Geometrics. I asked her what her choice would be, so that I could predict what her home was like and prove the theory. She chose a rectangle and a circle. I therefore surmised that as a rectangle she was probably in rented accommodation. She was perhaps thinking of changing jobs, so would not want roots and certainly not the financial commitment of a mortgage. As a circle, she would like comfort but, with little money to achieve it, she would add possibly a brightly covered throw over an aged sofa and add plants to cheer up worn wallpaper. Apparently, this was so accurate that she thought I had visited her home.

Two: The approach

When I was in San Francisco a number of years ago at a conference, I had the pleasure of meeting a diplomat who had participated in the SALT peace talks. He told a wonderful story about how the negotiations were concluded swiftly after all those years of Cold War.

Apparently after long, tedious spells of arguing over the smallest details, manoeuvring to score an advantage for the Americans over the Russians and vice versa, both sides would take a break to discuss their next game plan. The two nations were positioned at either end of an internal garden in the centre of a hotel. Both had balconies and could view each other from a distance across this atrium.

One day, at the end of a particularly enervating session, they retired to their respective rooms to plan the following day. One of the American party looked at the Russians on their side of the garden doing exactly the same as they were – brainstorming ideas, trying to outflank the opposition, beating them into submission. Tiredly he asked the group what they thought the Russians would want out of the next series of talks. They listed about 98 points on a flipchart. 'Why don't we work out what we will have to concede to them in the end and just give it to them now?' They felt they would have to give in on 96 of the 98 issues they had brainstormed but there were two major ones they had negotiated in some detail – arms proliferation and something else I can't remember.

You can imagine the Russians' faces when the Americans said they would capitulate on all but two of the issues. Negotiating these took considerably less time and before we knew it Gorbachev and Reagan were on the White House lawn shaking hands and signing treaties. A sight unthinkable only a few years before.

This way of working is now called the 'Harvard negotiation' (I call it the 'balcony approach' here) and is used throughout the world in places like South Africa. Many books have been written about these high-level talks but little about how we can use this technique in our more mundane but equally important dealings with others. So let me outline the 'balcony approach' for you more simply:

1. Go to your balcony.
2. Step to their side.

3. Invite them to step to your side.
4. Build a connecting bridge.

What does all this mean for us – especially for the difficult people in our lives?

First, it means that in tackling anyone who is not being agreeable we must look at what is going on and what part, if any, we play in their behaviour. So 'going to the balcony' is reminding us to assess and analyse both sides of the situation before jumping in with both feet.

Then 'the approach' recommends that we step to their side first, understand their story, even state verbally that we know where they are coming from. Because we are so tied up with our own agendas, we imagine that to win through we must stun them with our carefully honed arguments. We forget that to influence we must attend to the other person's motivation first. Why should they agree to anything we ask if there is nothing in it for them?

The 'what's in it for them' or WIFT factor is crucial to this style of negotiation. The Russians would never have agreed to a speedy deal if, up front, there were not huge advantages for them. 'Ah,' I hear you cry, 'so you just have to sell out your own principles to make this work'. No, because once you have stepped to their side and got a handle on these WIFT factors you invite them to see things from your point of view. After that negotiate, negotiate. Let's consider a practical example.

Example

You are out in the car for the day with three children in the back seat. You stop for petrol and three little voices proclaim 'I want to go to the toilet'. Unfortunately you are told that the station's toilets are out of order but it is suggested you visit the garage across the road.

There you meet that wonderful institution – 'more than my job's worth'. This attendant says that the manager has said not to let anyone use the facilities who has not purchased petrol. The attendant is intransigent.

How do you convince this person to let the children into the toilet as quickly as possible?

Imagine for a moment that they are your children and that you have to get them into the toilet past that difficult person or you are going to have an accident in the back seat of your car. You have about two minutes to negotiate. What would you do? What strategies would you employ for swift access?

- Would you be terribly nice and hope that the garage attendant was pleasant in return? OR
- Would you try to win and threaten with a letter to the manager? OR
- Would you buy something – oil, sweets to keep them happy?

The balcony approach suggests that when we assess the WIFT factor for our garage attendant, we find that it is to keep his job. When you say something, anything in the region of 'I don't want you to lose your job of course but I do have to get these children to the toilet. What do you suggest?', you can then brainstorm solutions that suit both parties.

The other great advantage of having a strategy for these situations is that you can plan your interactions in advance. I know these contretemps just happen out of the blue, but even if you mess it up at the time you can plan the return match and then use a different tack.

Three: Coping with anger and conflict

Sadly our relations with certain people have become too entrenched for negotiation, or emotions may be running too high. Time for another strategy. But first let's see how you handle negative emotion. Complete the 'What's the threat?' questionnaire, remembering to think of specific instances when you felt angry. You don't have to answer every question as it may not be your particular response.

What's the threat?

1. When do I usually keep quiet when I'm angry?

2. When do I usually walk away from the other person when I'm angry?

3. When have I simmered for days and then vented my anger in a big blow up?

4. When do I appear to be hurt when I'm actually angry?

5. When do I take my anger out on someone other than the person who caused the anger?

6. When have I expressed my anger directly and firmly but without calling the other person names?

7. When someone else is angry with me, when do I respond directly and effectively, with composure? Can I listen and try to understand their grievances?

8. When do I feel hurt and withdrawn when someone is angry with me?

Anger is such a disruptive emotion, yet we all feel it at some time. How we handle anger is key to handling difficult people. Goleman talks about 'emotional hijacking', where anger takes over and rationality flies out the window. We keep quiet when we should talk, walk away when we should stay, simmer when we should ventilate and when we do let it out it is usually at the wrong people. And when others are angry with us, I am not sure we handle that interaction any better.

Take a look at your answers to see what you should be working on. The ideal is an ability to talk about how you feel without raising your voice or losing the place. The DESC script below is wonderful for very clear communication without losing your temper.

DESC – describe, emotion, solutions, consequences

It looks deceptively simple, but its use will help you to communicate clearly and directly as well as prolonging your life through reducing the stress of handling difficult people. The DESC script is:

- ■ *Describe* the behaviour that is affecting you. Be clear and use any evidence that will support your argument.
- ■ *Emotion*. Talk about how you feel, whether irritated, angry, enraged or unhappy.
- ■ *Solutions*. Discuss what can be done or what you would like to have done to improve the situation.
- ■ *Consequences*. Suggest what might result if the behaviour is not improved, and the positives that could result if changes were made.

There are many people who have rarely or possibly never been given feedback about their behaviour, and you may be the first to do so. Those who bully or use aggressive behaviour can get away with it for a long time. Having worked with the most difficult and challenging people, I now realize that they do not plan to be obstructive. It's not as if they wake up each day and wonder who they can mess up or shout at. As often as not they have no idea how they come across and certainly no idea how much power they weald. If only they knew that if they just whispered, most would rush to their bidding. They really do need the feedback.

The essentials of the DESC script are:

- ■ *Describe*. You must precisely describe your difficult person's behaviour to them, face to face. I remember being referred a client with the words, 'This man needs a personality transplant'. Now how helpful is that? It certainly didn't enable this person to change or provide me with any concrete objectives. Also, if you have any evidence of bad or inappropriate behaviour, now is the time to produce it. Time sheets if they have been late, reports of aggressive incidents – any feedback that moves your discussion on from hearsay and gossip. Remember that these people are very good at defending themselves and maintaining the status quo, so collect your ammunition well in advance.

- *Emotion.* You must remember to talk about how you feel. This is such powerful feedback, especially if you have been trying to effect change for a while. You may feel that it puts you in a vulnerable position to do so, but believe me it does not. The majority of people I have dealt with don't wish to cause mayhem and upset and this leverage can inspire change. I remember a girl on one of my courses whose sister infuriated her. She would spend the weekend in her flat, have wild parties to which she was never invited, and then leave the detritus for her to clear up. In the past she would swing from being silently martyred to having screaming arguments. This time she used the DESC script and talked about how her sister's behaviour made her feel: left out, exhausted and martyred, with an overwhelming desire never to invite her again. The sister was nonplussed to say the least. She had thought her sister hated her friends and so had never thought to include her. They had never helped with the cleaning because it was always completed by the time they surfaced. Solutions were negotiated and when she last wrote to me there had been a lasting peace.

- *Solutions.* If it is a work situation, you may want your member of staff to write down his or her negotiated solutions. A lot of the compliance work carried out with GPs would suggest that if they asked us to write down how to take our medication, there would be less half-empty bottles on shelves and less persistent infection around. I have yet to meet a GP who has done this, but it is a nice thought. However, we can make use of this research and have paper and pen handy.

- *Consequences.* Many people have little idea about the consequences of their behaviour. Perhaps they were just given things as children, instead of earning them, or constantly charmed their way out of scrapes. You may be the first person to talk about what will happen to them if they continue to behave in the same way. It would be very positive to point out the good consequences that would ensue should their behaviour change in the desired direction.

The last essentials are to provide a timescale for improvement and to monitor progress. If the practised difficult person knows that nothing will be followed-up, then he or she will not be motivated to change. It goes without saying that even the most minuscule movement in the right direction should be rewarded. If no one notices, why bother! If the right changes are not forthcoming, then retarget till they do.

The power of the DESC script lies in its directness. It is sharp, focused and you can remain relaxed as you communicate clearly how you feel. Why should your life be shortened by someone else's stupid behaviour?

To return to directness for a moment, so many managers have told me over the years how they are going to give a certain member of staff a 'flea in their ear' or 'a piece of their mind' or some other epithet. The reality is that when you meet that employee afterwards and ask how the interview went, he or she will tell you that they discussed holidays and football but the manager only talked vaguely about the work bit. In other words, giving bad news is never easy and we often try to sugar-coat it. This process so dilutes the interaction that the core message is lost. We may think we have had the conversation, while the recipient hasn't a clue. DESC allows you to be direct and stick to the point no matter what.

The script is just as good for letters too. I am about to write to a computer company to complain that they have charged me twice for the same item. So writing this will remind me to use the DESC script to hone my argument and retrieve my money.

When someone is angry with you, it so easy to become defensive and fight fire with fire. In this process we lose sight of our purpose, which is usually to get the other person to listen to us. If we want to be truly effective, instead of just winning the point, then we must find a way of admitting to what is correct in our protagonist's argument. To prove this – have you ever tried arguing with someone who is agreeing with you? You just can't for any sustained period. I had this demonstrated to me by a fellow psychologist, Bob Sharpe, who introduced me to the concept. He asked me to role-play extreme anger with him. It was a cathartic moment. You are not often given carte blanche to be as nasty as you like. Then he cleverly started to agree with me, not with everything, but selectively. I tried in vain to summon my previous harridan-like behaviour to no avail. I just could not do it.

I have used the technique often at work and it's really effective. One word of caution though. You must be genuine in your agreement, as adversaries smell artifice at a hundred yards. That is why you must be selective. No need to agree with any personal abuse that is hurled at you.

Let's not forget the purpose of calming the other person down. It is to resolve the conflict. So just like the DESC script, get to solutions quickly. What would they like you to do to fix the problem?

Four: Positive outcomes

So often with those difficult or challenging people we get into a mindset that allows nothing they do to be any good. They breathe and we are irritated. If you are going to embark on a policy of improving the situation, then you must start to envisage positive outcomes. If we visualize how we would like them to be, then we can steer them in the right direction. You might want to share that vision with them so that you both have a goal to work towards.

The whole process of being positive has a relaxing effect, so your hot button is less likely to be triggered. You may never love your difficult people, but you can work with them.

Still trying to understand your difficult person, even at this stage, can help you reach agreement. A taxi driver picked me up from the airport and said he recognized my name. I had never seen him before. To aid my memory he explained that he picked me up each day from my flat (he named the street), took me into my office (he named the company), waited for me at night, sometimes for an hour before taking me home. And he had been doing this for some months. Suddenly I knew who this was. A former employee, who had brown hair like mine and on a dark night could have been taken for me, lived and worked now at those addresses. Back at the office with the accountant, we reviewed our taxi account print out. There was my name, but her telephone number. Of course we immediately changed the password and I made an appointment to see her, with some trepidation.

Well, she was a very good actress and admitted to nothing for about half an hour. It must be a mistake, it wasn't her, the taxi company were at fault. She was impressive despite my best efforts with the DESC script. I felt deflated and started to summarize the evidence. I remember saying that I could perhaps understand why it had happened. She had just bought a flat and so had possibly sold her car. I was sure she had not started out to use our taxi service every day, but when she had got away with it her usage had escalated. Suddenly she burst into tears, admitted to everything, and gave me a cheque for the entire amount.

This incident taught me a lot about human behaviour and a quote I came across recently encapsulated my thinking. Stephen Covey uses it to describe one of his seven habits. It is: 'Seek first to understand then to be understood'. Perhaps that sums up this book.

Of course there are no cast iron guarantees with these skills, but using them significantly increases the chances of getting what you want or communicating your point of view. As with the rest of the book, these techniques are to be used with elegance, a relaxed style, a focus on fostering great relationships and helping others achieve what they want.

Practising is important and you may feel uncomfortable at first. Do not let that put you off. I was using the FORE exercise with a client recently and he described his first attempts at taking the initiative socially as 'clunky'. However, he persevered and now he uses these skills automatically like breathing.

Since I first launched the concept of Impact, Thought, Emotion, and Action, this process of change has been used many times during the coaching of numerous people. But more publicly my change model was the one of choice for *Confidence Lab* on BBC2 and was also put to the test on six business people in *Confidence Zone* on *BBC Learning Zone*. If you are an insomniac or a shift worker, you can still view these programmes at ungodly hours of the morning on *BBC Learning Zone* or BBC World. Better still, buy the coaching package from the BBC and get a good night's sleep!

Most of the time the challenge from the BBC was to change people to be, for example, more assertive, less angry, more confident, less phobic, and they gave me one day per person per problem. Occasionally it occurred to me that it might not work this time, but I dismissed such thoughts as negative and I have to say the process has not yet let me down. Of course people are kick-started in that day and they have to continue the good work, but each person has been followed up and each has remained significantly changed. Of course some change more than others and that is down to individual differences and level of motivation. But change they all have.

Remember it takes three weeks to establish a new piece of behaviour and another nine weeks to turn that new behaviour into a habit. So repetition is important–repetition is important!

What I find spectacular about some people I have worked with is that once they have mastered one aspect or difficulty they then go on to use their new skills to master even more challenging problems.

Mary was frightened to drive to her daughter's and had not driven in her car for six years. When I saw her for a programme called *So You Think You're a Good Driver* she ended our session – a day as usual – by driving by herself to her daughter's house with the camera crew travelling behind trying to keep up with her. She also had fears about bursting balloons which stopped her going to parties and was so terrified of fireworks that she had to hide on 5 November. Not only did she conquer her balloon fears but she went on to enjoy her first firework display ever.

So be experimental and try out the skills. Then keep practising. Let me know of your successes. E-mail me at info@rostaylor.com.

Step 4 checklist

1. Use FORE anywhere – bus stops, stations, airport lounges – to establish relationships. Good relationships ease our path through life.
2. Invest in some emotional banking. When you become proactive in finding points of common interest it is difficult to be bored.
3. Handle difficult people elegantly by:
   analysing that difficult person;
   analysing yourself and what part you play;
   adopting a more negotiative approach;
   becoming skilled at dealing with anger and conflict;
   focusing on positive outcomes.
4. If this doesn't work, move on to the DESC script.

Key learning points

Now rerun the chapter and list, in Table 4.2, as specifically as possible, all the points that you wish to remember to put into practice.

Table 4.2   Key learning points

Key learning points that I found particularly useful from Chapter 4	How I intend to put these into practice
1.	
2.	
3.	
4.	
5.	

Further reading from Kogan Page

The Advanced Numeracy Test Workbook, Mike Bryon (2003)

Aptitude Personality and Motivation Tests: Assess Your Potential and Plan Your Career, 2nd edition, Jim Barrett (2004)

The Aptitude Test Workbook, Jim Barrett (2003)

The A–Z of Careers and Jobs, 12th edition, Susan Hodgson (2005)

Better Business Writing, Timothy V Foster (2002)

Boost Your Self-Esteem, John Caunt (2002)

Career, Aptitude and Selection Tests: Match Your IQ, Personality and Abilities to Your Ideal Career, Jim Barrett (1998)

Communicate to Win, Richard Denny (2001)

Dealing with Difficult People, Roy Lilley (2001)

Develop Your Assertiveness, 2nd edition, Sue Bishop (2000)

Develop Your NLP Skills, Andrew Bradbury (2000)

Developing Your Staff, Patrick Forsyth (2001)

E-business Essentials, Matt Haig (2001)

The Effective Leader, Rupert Eales-White (2003)

Empowering People, 2nd edition, Jane Smith (2000)

The First-Time Manager: The First Steps to a Brilliant Career, 3rd edition, Michael Morris (2005)

Graduate Job-Hunting Guide, Mark Parkinson (2001)

The Graduate Psychometric Test Workbook, Mike Bryon (2005)

Great Answers to Tough Interview Questions, 6th edition, Martin Yate (2005)

A Guide to Working for Yourself, revised 23rd edition, Jonathan Reuvid (2005)

How I Made It: 40 Successful Entrepreneurs Reveal All, Rachel Bridge (2004)

How People Tick: A Guide to Difficult People and How to Handle Them, Mike Leibling (2005)

How to be an Even Better Manager: A Complete A to Z of Proven Techniques & Essential Skills, Michael Armstrong (2004)

How to Manage Meetings, Alan Barker (2002)

How to Master Personality Questionnaires, 2nd edition, Mark Parkinson (2000)

How to Master Psychometric Tests, 3rd edition, Mark Parkinson (2004)

How to Motivate People, Patrick Forsyth (2000)

How to Pass Advanced Aptitude Tests, Jim Barrett (2002)

How to Pass Advanced Numeracy Tests, Mike Bryon (2002)

How to Pass Firefighter Recruitment Tests, Mike Bryon, (2004)

How to Pass Graduate Psychometric Tests, 2nd edition, Mike Bryon (2001)

How to Pass Numeracy Tests, 2nd edition, Harry Tolley & Ken Thomas (2000)

How to Pass Numerical Reasoning Tests: A Step-by Step Guide to Learning the Basic Skills, Heidi Smith (2003)

How to Pass Professional Level Psychometric Tests: Contains Practice Tests for IT, Management and Finance Recruitment, 2nd edition, Sam Al-Jajjoka (2004)

How to Pass Secondary School Selection Tests, Mike Bryon (2004)

How to Pass Selection Tests, 3rd edition, Mike Bryon & Sanjay Modha (2005)

How to Pass Technical Selection Tests, 2nd edition, Mike Bryon & Sanjay Modha (2005)

How to Pass the Civil Service Qualifying Tests, 2nd edition, Mike Bryon (2003)

How to Pass Verbal Reasoning Tests, 2nd edition, Harry Tolley & Ken Thomas (2000)

How to Succeed at an Assessment Centre: Test-Taking Advice from the Experts, 2nd edition, Harry Tolley & Robert Wood (2005)

How to Write a Business Plan, Brian Finch (2001)

How to Write a Marketing Plan, 2nd edition, John Westwood (2000)

How You Can Get That Job: Application Forms and Letters Made Easy, 3rd edition, Rebecca Corfield (2002)

Improve Your Communication Skills, Alan Barker (2000)

IQ and Psychometric Test Workbook, Philip Carter (2005)

IQ and Psychometric Tests, Philip Carter (2004)

The Leader's Guide to Lateral Thinking Skills: Powerful Problem-solving Techniques to Ignite Your Team's Potential, Paul Sloane (2003)

Motivate to Win, 3rd edition, Richard Denny (2005)

Organise Yourself, John Caunt (2000)

Powerful Reports and Proposals, Patrick Forsyth (2003)

Preparing Your Own CV: How to Improve your Chances of Getting The Job You Want, 3rd edition, Rebecca Corfield (2003)

Readymade CVs: Sample CVs for Every Type of Job, 3rd edition, Lynn Williams (2004)

Readymade Job Search Letters: Every Type of Letter for Getting the Job you Want, 3rd edition, Lynn Williams (2004)

Selling to Win, 3rd edition, Richard Denny (2006)

Shut Up & Listen!: The Truth about How to Communicate at Work, Theo Theobald and Cary Cooper (2004)

Start Up and Run Your Own Business, 4th edition, Jonathan Reuvid (2005)

Stay Confident, John Caunt (2001)

Succeed for Yourself: Unlock Your Potential for Achieving Success and Happiness, 3rd edition, Richard Denny (2006)

Successful Interview Skills: How to Present Yourself with Confidence, 4th edition, Rebecca Corfield (2006)

Successful Presentation Skills, 2nd edition, Andrew Bradbury (2000)

Successful Time Management, Patrick Forsyth (2003)

Team Building, Robert Maddux (2000)

The Ultimate Career Success Workbook: Tests and Exercises to Assess your Skills and Potential, Rob Yeung (2002)

The Ultimate CV Book: Write the Perfect CV and Get That Job, Martin Yate (2002)

The Ultimate Interview Book, Lynn Williams (2005)

The Ultimate Job Search Letters Book: Write a Perfect Letter and Get That Job, Martin Yate (2003)